W9-CPF-791

781.423 VOG
Vogler, Leonard.
How to read music /

OCT   2002

W 11/04   W 10/18
W 10/09
W 8/12
W 8/15

PROPERTY OF CLPL

Pocket Manual Series:

How To Read Music

by Len Vogler

All you need to know about major and minor key signatures; tempo and dynamic markings; ornaments, accents, and articulations; and much, much more.

Cover photography by SuperStock
Project editor: Peter Pickow
Interior design and layout: Len Vogler

This book Copyright © 2000 by Amsco Publications,
A Division of Music Sales Corporation, New York

All rights reserved. No part of this book may be
reproduced in any form or by any electronic or mechanical means,
including information storage and retrieval systems,
without permission in writing from the publisher.

Order No. AM 948960
US International Standard Book Number: 0.8256.1715.4
UK International Standard Book Number: 0.7119.7603.1

Exclusive Distributors:
Music Sales Corporation
257 Park Avenue South, New York, NY 10010 USA
Music Sales Limited
8/9 Frith Street, London W1V 5TZ England
Music Sales Pty. Limited
120 Rothschild Street, Rosebery, Sydney, NSW 2018, Australia

Printed in the United States of America by
Vicks Lithograph and Printing Corporation

Amsco Publications
New York/London/Paris/Sydney/Copenhagen/Madrid

Contents

The Basics

Pitch

When we hear sounds we usually relate to them as being high or low, like the low moaning of a foghorn or the high piercing sound of a siren. The height and/or depth of these sounds is called *pitch*. In scientific terms, pitch is the number of vibrations per second produced by a sound. In the example below, the first illustration is what middle C would look like played by a piano and the second illustration is what C above middle C would look like. Notice: the more vibrations there are, the higher the pitch.

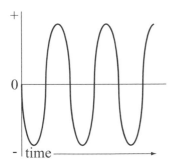 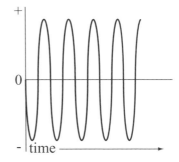

Since it would be difficult to use these waveforms as a way to read pitch, in any musical sense, a language of *notes* is used to make it easier to read and to understand. Musical notation provides the musician with a means to interpret each note or pitch.

Pitch can be either *relative* or *absolute*. Relative pitch of a tone is its position (higher or lower) as compared with that of another tone (see "Intervals" chapter). Absolute pitch is the fixed position of an entire range of musical tones.

The number of vibrations establishes the absolute pitch of a note. For example, in the United States, 440 vibrations per second produces an A note, commonly called *A440*. In Europe, the standard pitch is called *French* or *International*. Unlike the United States, the European pitch is 435 vibrations per second to produce an A note (or *A435*).

The Staff

The *staff* (or *stave* in the United Kingdom) is the basis for the language of written music. It consists of five parallel lines and four spaces.

In order for the eye to recognize pitch easily, the staff is laid out in this five-line format, but there are more tones or pitches than can fit on one staff. So, to determine what series of pitches will be on a given staff, a *clef symbol* is used.

The Treble Clef

The *treble clef* is used for the notation of music for middle or high instruments and voices. This clef is also known as the *G clef*, because the symbol encircles the second line from the bottom of the staff to indicate the position of the G note.

←—G line

The Bass Clef

The *bass clef* is used for low instruments and voices. This clef is also known as the *F clef* because the two dots to the right of the symbol indicate the position of the F note.

←—F line

The Alto Clef

The *alto clef* is for medium-ranged instruments and voices. This clef points to middle C; that is, the symbol's two outer curves come to a point on the third line of the staff to indicate the C note. The alto clef is a *moveable clef,* it can be moved up and down to change the starting point for the C note. The other two clefs in the example below are also known as *tenor* and *soprano clefs.*

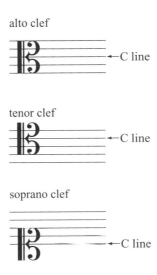

alto clef

←C line

tenor clef

←C line

soprano clef

←C line

The Grand Staff

Most music is written on a single staff. The pitch of the instrument or voice determines which clef is used. The treble clef is used by instruments like the violin, flute, clarinet, trumpet, and oboe. The alto clef is used by the viola, and the bass clef is used by string bass, bassoon, and tuba. There is one instrument that uses its own staff—the piano (also referred to as the *keyboard*). The piano is written on two staves that are bracketed together. The upper staff (or treble clef) is usually played by the right hand, and the lower staff or bass clef is usually played by the left hand. This combination of two staves is known as the *grand staff.*

Normally the grand staff is configured with the treble (or G) clef as the upper staff and the bass (or F) clef as the lower staff. These staves can also be both treble, or both bass, as well.

Notes

Notes are the foundation of the musical language. Notes provide two important pieces of information. First is pitch—how high or how low the note will sound—and second is duration—how long the note will last (although, as you will see later, there are other symbols that can also effect note duration). Notes are written on *either* a line or a space.

Notes are named using the first seven letters of the alphabet: A, B, C, D, E, F, and G. These note names are in ascending order— low to high. (If you were to go from high to low the order would be reversed—G, F, E, D, C, B, A.) Since there are only seven letters in the sequence, once G is reached the sequence repeats— A, B, C, D, E, F, G; A, B, C, D, E, F, G; A, B, C, D, E, F, G; and so on.

Notes on a Staff

In the example below you will notice the notes are placed in the treble clef, starting with D and continuing up to G. Every line and space is used and the notes follow one after another. Just as in reading text, you start at the left and read to the right, playing one note, then the next. At the end of a line, you go to the next line and continue as before.

Notes on the Treble Clef

Notes on the Bass Clef

Notes on the Alto Clef

Remembering the Names of the Notes

There are several ways to remember note names; one is by sheer repetition, the other is by using word phrases. The note names for the lines of the treble clef are E, G, B, D, F; so, using the first letter of each line the word phrase could be **Every Good Boy Does Fine.** You don't have to use this phrase exactly—you can make up your own. The spaces in the treble clef don't need a word phrase because they spell out a word—**FACE.**

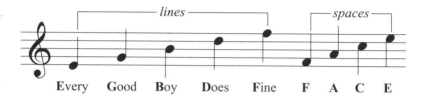

Every   Good   Boy   Does   Fine   F   A   C   E

The word phrase for the lines in the bass clef could be **Good Boys Do Fine Always,** and for the spaces—**All Cows Eat Grass.**

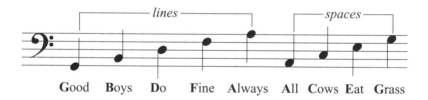

Good   Boys   Do   Fine   Always   All   Cows   Eat   Grass

Leger Lines

What happens when notes are added above or below the staff of five lines and four spaces? A system of small lines, the width of a note, is incorporated to extend the range of notes beyond (above or below) the staff. These lines are called *leger lines.* Leger lines are used for the same purpose in all clefs. The system of leger lines avoids the constant clutter of adding more lines and spaces, or clef changes (which makes music harder to read). The example below illustrates what a staff would look like without leger lines. Actually, this system of eleven lines was once used—it is called the *Great Staff.* As you can see, it is pretty cumbersome to read.

←middle C

The examples below spell out the leger lines for the treble, bass, and alto clefs.

Treble clef

Bass clef

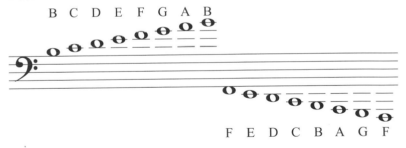

Alto clef

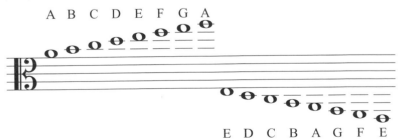

Octaves

We know that the note names start with A and end with G, and then start over again with A. The distance between the first A and the next A is eight notes, or an *octave*. Octave is the Greek word for "eight" and is a fundamental part of music study. The examples below demonstrate octaves.

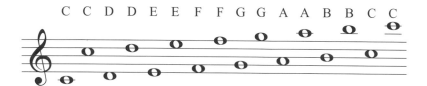

Play a C on the piano and count up eight note names and play the other C—one octave above. You will notice that they sound *almost* the same, but the C an octave above sounds *higher.* That's because the higher C is producing twice as many vibrations as the C an octave lower. If you play both Cs together you will notice they resemble each other.

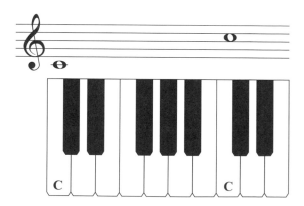

The Octave Sign

To avoid excessive use of leger lines in very high or very low passages, the octave sign (8va) may be used. The octave sign is an abbreviation of the Italian phrase meaning "at the octave":

all'ottava. If placed above notes in the treble staff, it means to play those notes one octave higher. If placed below notes in the bass clef (sometimes with the additional clarification *bassa*), it means to play those notes one octave lower. The octave sign may be extended to apply to several notes by following it with a dotted line as in the following examples.

written:

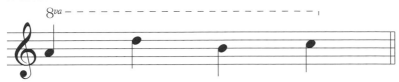

notes played:

written:

notes played:

Sometimes the word *loco* ("place" in Italian) is placed at the end of an *all'ottava* passage to alert the player that the notes should be played as written from that point on.

13

Rhythm and Note Values

Rhythm

Rhythm, simply stated, is the "time" of the music. *Beat, stress,* and *tempo* or *speed* are all terms that refer to rhythm. The rhythm of a piece may be specified as rigid and structured, loose and free-flowing, or may be left to the interpretation of a musician or conductor. Rhythm is a series of values that can be placed in any combination for endless possibilities. Mastering rhythm is essential to the study of music.

Note Values

In the previous chapter you learned how notes relate to pitch—that is, how *high* or *low* a note sounds. Notes also have *note value* or *duration*—how long the note lasts. The *beat* is how the duration of a note is counted. The beat provides the basic structure for rhythm. The beat is the pulse in music that divides time equally, like the ticking of your watch or the beating of your heart.

The following chart shows six of the most common notes and their duration or *beat count.*

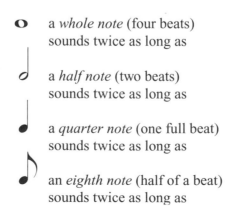

a *whole note* (four beats)
sounds twice as long as

a *half note* (two beats)
sounds twice as long as

a *quarter note* (one full beat)
sounds twice as long as

an *eighth note* (half of a beat)
sounds twice as long as

a *sixteenth note* (quarter of a beat)
sounds twice as long as

a *thirty-second note* (eighth of a beat)

The United Kingdom uses the same notes, but different note names.

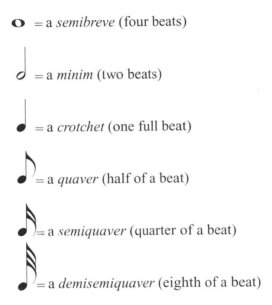

O = a *semibreve* (four beats)

= a *minim* (two beats)

= a *crotchet* (one full beat)

= a *quaver* (half of a beat)

= a *semiquaver* (quarter of a beat)

= a *demisemiquaver* (eighth of a beat)

The half note and the quarter note consist of a note head and a stem.

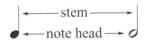

The written eighth note has the same elements as the half note and quarter note, but it also has a flag.

15

The sixteenth note has two flags.

The thirty-second note has three flags. For each subdivision of the note add another flag.

When eighth notes, sixteenth notes, and thirty-second notes are grouped in consecutive order they are often joined together by beams. The number of beams is determined by the number of flags of a particular note. The following chart shows how these notes are beamed.

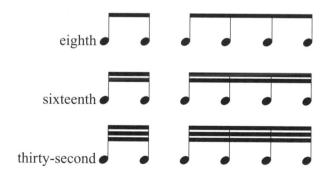

This chart shows how note values relate to one another.

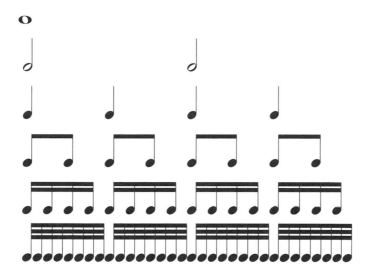

Rests

Rests are the silence in music. Notes indicate the sound, and rests indicate silence. Just like notes, rests are counted in beats and are named after their note counterpart. The chart below shows the notes and their equivalent rest.

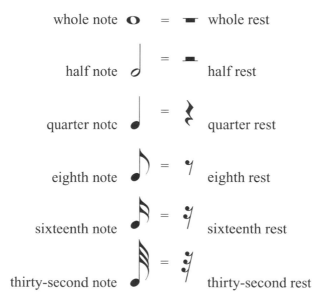

17

The following example demonstrates how notes and rests can be combined on a staff.

In order to comprehend the principle of rests more easily, try this: In the following example, count the beats out loud (1 2 3 4 in each measure) while you clap only for the notes, leaving silence for the rests.

Dotted Notes

When a dot is placed after a note or rest it increases the value of the note by one-half and is called a *dotted note.* For example, a dotted half note receives three beats—two beats for the half note and one for the dot.

A dot after a rest also increases its value by one-half.

This chart shows the notes and dotted notes, and how many beats each receives. Memorize the values for the dotted notes and rests.

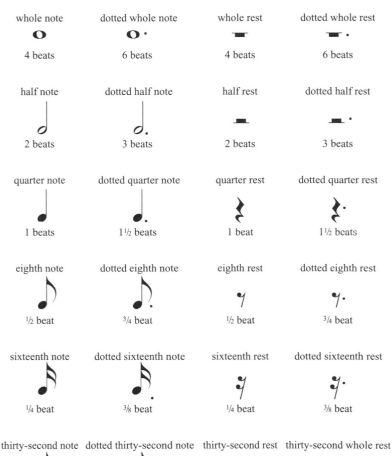

whole note	dotted whole note	whole rest	dotted whole rest
O	**O** ·	▬	▬ ·
4 beats	6 beats	4 beats	6 beats

half note	dotted half note	half rest	dotted half rest
2 beats	3 beats	2 beats	3 beats

quarter note	dotted quarter note	quarter rest	dotted quarter rest
1 beats	1½ beats	1 beat	1½ beats

eighth note	dotted eighth note	eighth rest	dotted eighth rest
½ beat	¾ beat	½ beat	¾ beat

sixteenth note	dotted sixteenth note	sixteenth rest	dotted sixteenth rest
¼ beat	⅜ beat	¼ beat	⅜ beat

thirty-second note	dotted thirty-second note	thirty-second rest	thirty-second whole rest
⅛ beat	3/16 beat	⅛ beat	3/16 beat

Measures and Barlines

You've seen how notes can be written on a staff by pitch and note value. These notes are then organized into groups called *measures*. Each measure will contain the same number of beats and is divided from the following measure by a thin vertical line called a *barline* (or simply a *bar*). The number and type of beats in each measure is determined by the time signature, which will be discussed in the "Time Signature" chapter.

A *double barline* (or *double bar*) is a thin vertical line parallel to a thick vertical line tells the musician where the music ends. A double barline that consists of two thin vertical lines is used to separate music into different sections

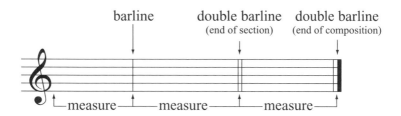

Stem Direction

The direction of the note stem is determined by the placement of the note on the staff. For notes that are written below the middle line of the staff, the stems point up. Notes from the middle line and above—stems point down. This rule applies to *all* clefs.

The direction of the majority of stems will determine how a group of eighth, sixteenth, and thirty-second notes will be beamed.

Where music is notated for two voices to sing (or for two instruments to play) simultaneously, the note stems will face up *and* down throughout a measure.

Accidentals

Accidentals

Until now we have only discussed notes that are represented by the white keys of the piano—A, B, C, D, E, F, and G. The notes on the black keys—the notes between A, B, C, D, E, F, and G—are called *accidentals*. Depending on their musical usage these notes are called *sharp notes* or *flat notes*. Sharp or flat notes are recognized by a symbol placed to the left of the note head; ♯ is a *sharp sign* and ♭ is a *flat sign*.

Sharps

A sharp note is named for the white key one half-step *below* it. For example, the note between D and E is D♯; the note between G and A is G♯. Notice that there are no sharps between B and C, or between E and F, although there are times that an F will be called E♯, and C will be called B♯ (see the section "Enharmonic Spelling" in the "Harmony" chapter).

A   A♯

Below is a chart of the sharp notes on the keyboard.

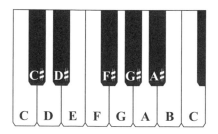

This is how the same sharp notes are written on a treble staff.

Here are the same notes written on the bass staff one octave lower.

Flats

A flat note is named for the white key one half-step *above* it. For example, the note between D and E is E♭; the note between G and A is A♭. You are probably wondering why there are two names for the same note. This question will be answered in the chapter "Key Signatures." Again. notice that there are no flats between B and C or between E and F, although there are times when an E will be called F♭ and a B will be called C♭ (see the section "Enharmonic Spelling" in the "Harmony" chapter).

Below is a chart of the flat notes on the keyboard.

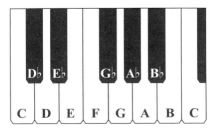

This is how the same notes are written on a treble staff.

Here are the same notes written on the bass staff one octave lower.

When a note is altered by either a sharp or flat, all following notes of the same pitch are similarly affected until the beginning of the next measure: the barline cancels the accidental's effect.

Even though the effect of an accidental is canceled by the barline, you will often see a *courtesy accidental* when a previously altered note appears in the subsequent measure. This type of reminder is especially called for when the first statement of the previously altered note is the first note of the following measure.

Naturals

The *natural sign* (♮) is used to cancel either a sharp or flat in the same position on the staff. After the natural sign is applied, all following notes of the same pitch will remain natural, unless a sharp or a flat is again introduced.

Sometimes you will encounter music that has both sharps and flats. As a general rule, notes leading *up* to the next notes are sharped and notes leading *down* are flatted.

Double Sharps

The *double sharp* (✗) raises a note by two half-steps, but if the note is already sharped, it is raised only by a half-step. You won't see this symbol very often, it is used mostly for visual continuity.

Double Flats

The *double flat* (♭♭) lowers a note by two half-steps, but if the note is already flatted, it is lowered by only a half-step.

Natural Sharps and Double Naturals

The *natural sharp* (♮♯) is used to lower a double sharp note to its sharp position—down one half-step. A *double natural* (♮♮) cancels either a double flat or a double sharp and returns the note to its original position—down or up two half-steps.

Natural Flats

The *natural flat* (♮♭) is used to raise a double flat note to its flat position—up one half-step.

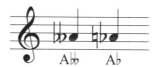

The natural sharp, natural flat, and double natural are rarely used today. A single sharp is more commonly used to cancel a double sharp note and make it a sharp note.

A single natural is commonly used to cancel either a double sharp or a double flat.

A single flat is commonly used to cancel a double flat note and make it a flat note.

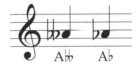

Intervals

Melody refers to an organized succession of tones. The difference in pitch between any two tones in a melody is called an *interval*. The smallest possible interval is called a *half step*. A half step corresponds to the difference in pitch between any two adjacent keys on a piano keyboard.

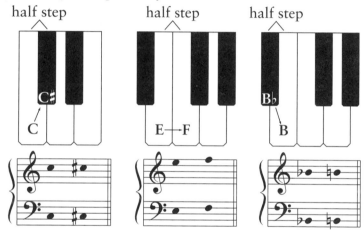

A *whole step* is equal to two half-steps. On the piano, a whole step covers the distance of three keys.

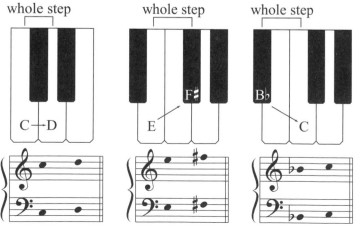

Half steps and whole steps are two basic types of intervals used when discussing the distance between neighboring notes in a melody or a scale. These are called *melodic intervals.*

When intervals are played *simultaneously* they are called *harmonic intervals.*

The following chart shows the names given to the different intervals.

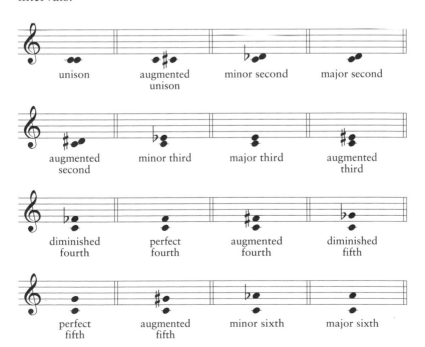

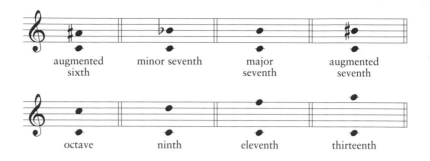

augmented sixth | minor seventh | major seventh | augmented seventh

octave | ninth | eleventh | thirteenth

Notice the minor second is the same as a half step and the major second is equal to a whole step.

Learning to identify harmonic intervals is a visual process. Once you've learned to recognize the intervals visually, you will be able to pick them out in any key. Use the following examples to memorize harmonic intervals.

second

contains one note on a line and one note on a space.

third

contains two notes on adjacent lines, or two notes on adjacent spaces.

fourth

contains one note on a line and one note on a space directly above the first note.

fifth

contains two notes on spaces with one space in between, or two notes on lines with one line in between.

sixth

contains one note on a line and one note on a space with two lines and two spaces in between.

seventh

contains two notes on two spaces with two spaces in between, or two notes on two lines with two lines in between.

octave

contains one note on a line and one note on a space with three spaces and three lines in between.

Time Signatures

The beat is the pulse of a musical composition, and the *time signature* regulates that pulse. The time signature provides two important pieces of rhythmic information. First, how many beats are in a measure and second, the value of a beat or note.

$\mathbf{2}$ = number of beats in a measure
$\mathbf{4}$ = the value of one beat

The time signature consists of two numbers. The top number determines how many beats there will be in a measure, and the bottom number tells you which type of note receives one beat. This chart shows the numeric equivalent for the whole, half, quarter, eighth, and sixteenth notes.

$\mathbf{1}$ = whole note
$\mathbf{2}$ = half note
$\mathbf{4}$ = quarter note
$\mathbf{8}$ = eighth note
$\mathbf{16}$ = sixteenth note

Simple Time Signatures

Time signatures are divided into two types—*simple* and *compound.* Simple time signatures are signatures whose top number is two, three, or four. The following are examples of simple time signatures.

$$\frac{2}{8} \quad \frac{3}{8} \quad \frac{4}{8} \quad \frac{2}{4} \quad \frac{3}{4} \quad \frac{4}{4} \quad \frac{2}{2} \quad \frac{3}{2} \quad \frac{4}{2}$$

⁴⁄₄ Time

As far as simple time signatures go, ⁴⁄₄ (pronounced "four-four") is the most commonly used and is sometimes referred to as *common time*. The symbol [**C**], for common time, is sometimes used instead of ⁴⁄₄.

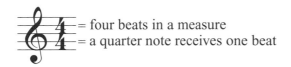
= four beats in a measure
= a quarter note receives one beat

= common time or ⁴⁄₄

Stressed and Unstressed Beats

Certain beats of a measure are *stressed* and others are *unstressed*. In ⁴⁄₄ the first and the third beats are stressed—the third beat to a lesser extent than the first—and beats two and four are unstressed. Although a time signature can suggest which notes are stressed and unstressed, the composer is not limited to where these stressed notes may be placed.

stressed   stressed

³⁄₄ Time

³⁄₄ (pronounced "three-four") is often called *waltz time,* because this time signature is used in many dance compositions. In ³⁄₄ the first beat is the *only* stressed beat.

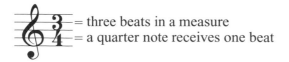
= three beats in a measure
= a quarter note receives one beat

$\frac{2}{4}$ Time

Most marches are in $\frac{2}{4}$ time. This is why $\frac{2}{4}$ is sometimes called *march time*. Every other beat in $\frac{2}{4}$ is stressed, giving it a **one**-two, **one**-two—or marching—feel.

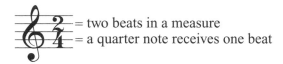

= two beats in a measure
= a quarter note receives one beat

Cut Time or $\frac{2}{2}$ Time

Until now you have only encountered time signatures where a quarter note gets one beat, but in $\frac{2}{2}$ a half note receives one beat. This is known as *cut time* and this symbol [₵] is often used instead of $\frac{2}{2}$.

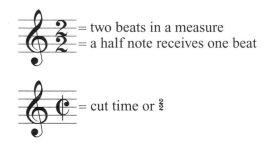

= two beats in a measure
= a half note receives one beat

= cut time or $\frac{2}{2}$

$\frac{3}{2}$ and $\frac{4}{2}$ Time

$\frac{3}{2}$ and $\frac{4}{2}$ time also have half notes that receive one beat and only the first beat of each measure is stressed.

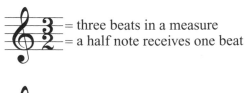

= three beats in a measure
= a half note receives one beat

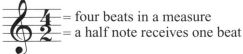

= four beats in a measure
= a half note receives one beat

⅜, ⅜, and ⁴⁄₈ Time

So far we have seen simple time signatures where quarter and half notes receive one beat. In ⅜, ⅜, and ⁴⁄₈ time an eighth note receives one beat. The first beat for all these time signatures is stressed.

stressed

stressed

stressed

Compound Time Signatures

In *compound time signatures* the top number is a multiple of three, also provides the stressed note information. The following are the most commonly used compound time signatures.

$$\frac{6}{16} \quad \frac{9}{16} \quad \frac{12}{16} \quad \frac{6}{8} \quad \frac{9}{8} \quad \frac{12}{8} \quad \frac{6}{4} \quad \frac{9}{4} \quad \frac{12}{4}$$

You read compound time signatures the same as you do the simple signature; the top number tells you the number of beats and the bottom number tells you the note value.

Take a look at this example in ⁶⁄₈: the stressed notes are boldfaced (notice the multiples of three).

Here are the other compound time signatures and their stressed notes.

Dotted notes play an important role in compound time—three notes are counted as one.
Here are the dotted note values for the most common compound time signatures.

37

Time signatures can also be categorized in the following way:

Simple Duple
All simple time signatures with two beats to a measure.

Simple Triple
All simple time signatures with three beats to a measure.

Simple Quadruple
All simple time signatures with four beats to a measure.

The dotted note or compound beat is used as the basis for naming compound time signatures.

Compound Duple
All compound time signatures with two compound beats to a measure.

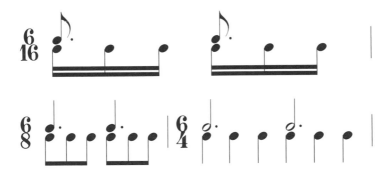

Compound Triple
All compound time signatures with three compound beats to a measure.

Compound Quadruple

All compound time signatures with four compound beats to a measure.

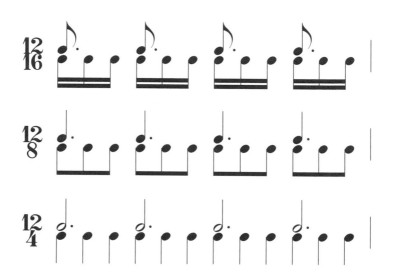

Complex Time Signatures

Along with simple and compound time signatures there are *complex time signatures,* like ⅝, ⅝, ⅞, and ⅞. The following examples indicate the most common stress patterns.

Tied Notes

A tie is a curved line that connects two or more notes of the same pitch. The tie indicates that you should hold the notes for the duration of their combined values.

Ties are often used between measures as in the example below.

Ties are also used to make the rhythm easier to read. As you can see in the example below, the dotted quarter is tied to the eighth showing the musician exactly where the beat count is in the measure. In the other example you can see how the beat count is obscured when the dotted quarter and eighth combination are replaced with a half note.

correct

incorrect

41

Ties can be used to hold a note over several measures.

When an accidental is used at the beginning of a series of tied notes, all following notes of the same pitch are affected by that accidental. If an altered note is tied across a barline, the tied note is also altered. However, any following notes of the same pitch are unaltered unless the accidental is repeated. A courtesy accidental is usually used in this situation.

A B C♯ (C♯) C B♭ (B♭) B A

Syncopation

When the melody stresses notes that are not on the beat, the rhythm is said to be *syncopated*. Syncopated rhythms may occur in any time signature; take a look at the examples below.

Triplets

Sometimes it becomes necessary to divide a note value into three equal parts. This is known as a *triplet*. Triplets are indicated by a *3* placed in the middle of the beam or bracket of the notes that make up the triplet. An easy way to remember how triplets work is to think of three notes in the same space as two of the same kind of note. Triplets can be made up of any note value, but they are most commonly used with quarter, eighth, and sixteenth notes.

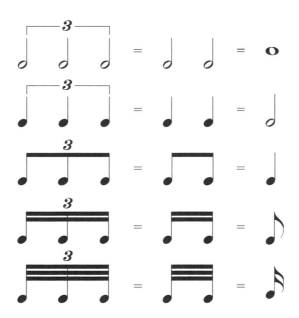

Duplets

When two notes receive the same time value as three notes, this is called a *duplet*. Duplets are used mostly in compound time signatures and are rarely used in popular music. Take a look at the example below in § time. Notice that the duplet in this signature has the value of three eighth-notes.

43

Quadruplets

A *quadruplet* consists of four notes played in the space of three of the same kind of note.

Quintuplets

A *quintuplet* is a group of five notes played in the space of four of the same kind of note.

Sextuplets

A *sextuplet* is a group of six notes played in the space of four of the same kind of note.

Septuplet

A *septuplet* is a group of seven notes played in the space of four of the same kind of note.

Scales

Scale Construction

Scales are the foundation on which most music is based. A scale is made up of a series of tones arranged in a specific interval pattern.

Major Scales

The quality of a scale—whether it is major, minor, etc.—is determined by the sequential arrangement of half steps and whole steps. The major scale has a half step between the third and fourth degrees, and another half step between the seventh and eighth degrees. All other scale steps are separated from their neighbors by a whole step. This arrangement of half steps and whole steps is the same for major scales in every key.

C major scale

It is common to refer to scale steps, or degrees, by Roman numerals and also by the following name:

    I. Tonic
   II. Supertonic
  III. Mediant
  IV. Subdominant
   V. Dominant
  VI. Submediant
 VII. Leading tone

Notice the relationship of these numbers to the naming of intervals (see "Interval" chapter).

I   II   III   IV   V   VI   VII   I

Minor Scales

There are three different types of minor scales: *natural (Aeolian), harmonic,* and *melodic.* All major scales have a corresponding *relative minor* scale. The minor scale can be determined by starting on the sixth step of any major scale. For example, start on the sixth step of a C scale and by playing each mahor scale note in succession (A B C D E F G) an A minor scale will be created. Therefore, A minor is the relative minor of C major. This scale is said to be *natural,* or *pure,* because it follows the major-scale formula without altering the key signature.

C major

A minor

A natural minor scale (Aeolian)

I   II   III   VI   V   VI   VII   I
(VIII)

The harmonic minor scale has half steps between scale steps *two* and *three, five* and *six,* and *seven* and *eight.* Notice: The distance between scale steps six and seven is a minor third.

A harmonic minor scale

The melodic minor scale's ascending order finds half steps between *two* and *three* and between *seven* and *eight.* Unlike any of the other scales that have been discussed so far, melodic minor scales have a different descending order. The descending order has half steps between degrees *six* and *five* and between *three* and *two*—with a whole step between steps *eight* and *seven.*

A melodic minor scale (ascending)

A melodic minor scale (descending)

Jazz Melodic Minor Scales

The jazz melodic minor scale is the same as the melodic minor
scale except that its descending pattern is the same as its
ascending pattern. The formula is whole step, half step,
whole step, whole step, whole step, whole step, and half step.

C jazz melodic minor scale

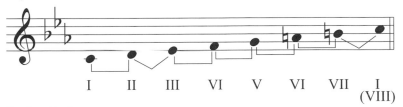

Dorian Scales

The Dorian scale begins on the second degree of the major scale.
The formula for the Dorian scale is whole step, half step,
whole step, whole step, whole step, half step, and whole step.
The Dorian scale resembles the natural minor scale with a raised
sixth.

D Dorian scale

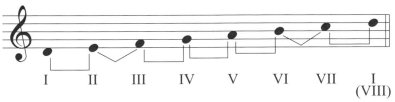

Phrygian Scales

The Phrygian scale begins on the third degree of the major scale.
The Phrygian scale formula is half step, whole step, whole step,
whole step, half step, whole step, and whole step. The Phrygian
scale resembles the natural minor scale with a lowered second.

E Phrygian scale

Lydian Scales

The Lydian scale begins on the fourth degree of the major scale. The formula for this scale is whole step, whole step, whole step, half step, whole step, whole step, and half step. The Lydian scale resembles the major scale with a raised fourth.

F Lydian scale

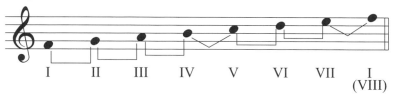

I   II   III   IV   V   VI   VII   I
(VIII)

Lydian Flat-Seven Scales

The Lydian flat-seven is just like the Lydian scale except that the seventh degree of the scale is lowered. The formula for this scale is whole step, whole step, whole step, half step, whole step, half step, and whole step.

F Lydian flat-seven scale

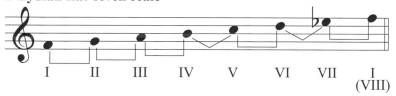

I   II   III   IV   V   VI   VII   I
(VIII)

Mixolydian Scales

The Mixolydian scale begins on the fifth degree of the major scale. The formula for this scale is whole step, whole step, half step, whole step, whole step, half step, and whole step. The Mixolydian scale resembles the major scale with a lowered seventh.

G Mixolydian scale

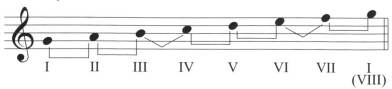

I   II   III   IV   V   VI   VII   I
(VIII)

Locrian Scales

The last mode is Locrian, which begins on the seventh degree of the major scale. The Locrian formula is half step, whole step, whole step, half step, whole step, whole step, and whole step. The Locrian scale resembles the natural minor scale with a lowered second and fifth.

B Locrian scale

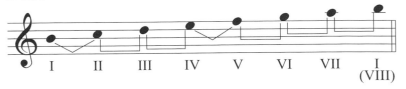

Pentatonic Major Scales

The pentatonic scales are five-note scales. These scales can be heard in the solos of many rock and blues players. The formula for the pentatonic major scale is whole step, whole step, minor third, whole step, and minor third.

C pentatonic scale

Pentatonic Minor Scales

The pentatonic minor is also a five-note scale. The formula for these scales is minor third, whole step, whole step, minor third, and whole step.

C pentatonic minor scale

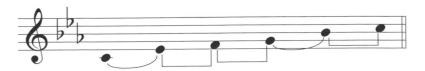

Blues Scales

The blues scale can be found in a variety of blues, rock, and jazz styles. The formula for this scale is minor third, half step, half step, half step, half step, minor third, and whole step.

C blues scale

For practical purposes, some musicians consider this blues scale to be two individual, complementary scales. These are often referred to as the *minor blues scale* and the *major blues scale*

C minor blues scale

C major blues scale

Notice that the major blues scale has the same relationship to the minor blues scale as a major scale has to its relative minor.

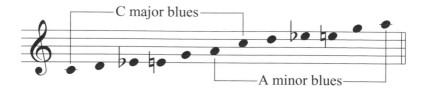

Whole-Tone Scales

The whole-tone scale has the simplest formula—it consists of all whole steps. Unlike traditional scales, the whole-tone scales do not contain basic intervals like the perfect fourth, perfect fifth, and the leading tone.

Impressionistic composers of the early twentieth century made use of whole-tone scales in their compositions.

C whole-tone scale

Key Signatures

Major Key Signatures

Now that you know how a C major scale is constructed, let's look at how this relates to other major scales. If you divide the C major scale in half, you will notice that both the first half and the second half use the same configuration of half steps and whole steps—and that the two halves are separated by a whole step. Since the half-step/whole-step formula is the same for both halves of the scale, and since all major scales use the same formula, you can construct a new scale that begins with the second half of the C major scale. The example below shows that the resulting scale will be a G major scale. Unlike the C major scale, which has no sharps or flats, the G major scale must always have an F♯ to make it conform to the major-scale formula of half steps and whole steps. Since the key of G major always contains an F♯, this F♯ appears in the *key signature* of G major.

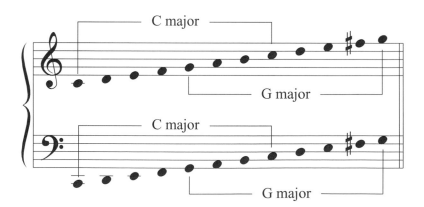

The key of G

Now, do the same thing with a G major scale that we did above with the C scale. The new scale starts on D and has two sharps: F♯ and C♯. As a result, the key signature for D major contains two sharps. Notice that with each new scale the seventh degree is sharped and this sharp is added to the right of the previous sharp (or sharps) in the key signature.

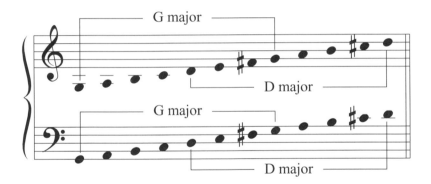

The key of D

Circle of Fifths

By now you have probably noticed a pattern developing; we take the fifth degree of a scale to start a new scale, and with each new scale we add a sharp. The chart below is referred to as the *circle of fifths*—it starts with C major and progresses around the circle by fifths through all the keys, ending back at C major. By using this chart you will be able to write and play all twelve major scales.

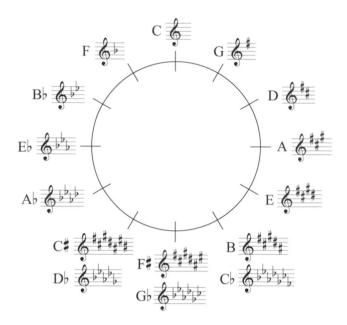

Here is an easy way to recognize sharp key signatures. Find the name of the last sharp in the signature and raise it one half step, this will give you the name of the major key.

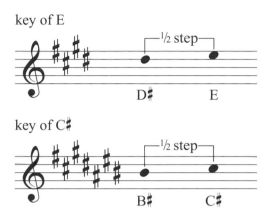

key of E

key of C♯

You will notice, in the circle of fifths chart, that the sharps are placed in a specific order on the staff for each key. Here is a way to remember how the sharps are placed on the staff for each key. The first sharp, for the key of G, is on the F line; this you will have to commit to memory. To place the second sharp, creating the key of D, count down three note positions to the C line. Placing a sharp on the C line will give you the necessary signature for playing in the key of D. Following the circle of fifths to the next key —A—you have to count up four note positions to G. This pattern can be used throughout the cycle, except for the key of B. If you were to follow this pattern the sharp for B would be on the A above the staff on a leger line. To avoid this the sharp is placed on the A, three note positions down from the D. The last two signatures, for F♯ and C♯, follow the pattern as before.

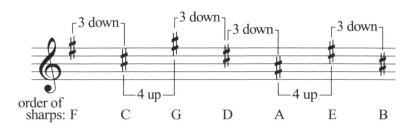

Here is an easy way to recognize flat key signatures. Find the name of the next to the last flat in the signature and this will give you the name of the key that the music is written in.

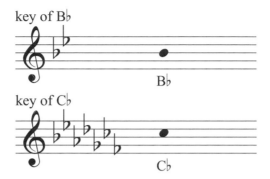

Just like the sharps, the flats are also in a specific order. The first flat is an alteration of the scale necessary to formulate the key of F. This flat is on the B line and, like the key of G, it will have to be memorized. Count up three note positions to E and place a flat in the E space for the key of B♭. Now count down four note positions to A for the key of E♭. Follow this pattern throughout the cycle for all the flatted keys.

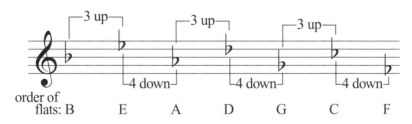

Minor Key Signatures

As stated earlier in this chapter, all major scales have a relative minor scale. Instead of using accidentals each time a minor scale is written it is easier to use key signatures. For example, the C natural minor scale has three flats—E♭, A♭, and B♭. These are the same flatted notes used in the E♭ major key signature, therefore C minor is the relative minor to E♭. Conversely, E♭ is known as the *relative major* of C minor. Accidentals are still required on the seventh degree of the C harmonic minor and on the sixth and seventh degree of the ascending C melodic minor scale.

Here are the three different forms of the minor scale notated without key signatures:

C natural minor

C harmonic minor

C melodic minor

Here are the minor scales notated with key signatures:

C natural minor

C harmonic minor

C melodic minor

Below is a list of all the major keys and their relative minor keys. See the appendix for the relative minor scales.

Major Key	Relative Minor
C	A minor
G	E minor
D	B minor
A	F♯ minor
E	C♯ minor
B	G♯ minor
F♯	D♯ minor
C♯	A♯ minor
F	D minor
B♭	G minor
E♭	C minor
A♭	F minor
D♭	B♭ minor
G♭	E♭ minor
C♭	A♭ minor

Harmony

Chords

Chords are produced by combining two or more intervals, and the simplest of these combinations is a *triad*. A triad consists of three notes obtained by the superposition of two thirds. The notes are called the root (or tonic), the third, and the fifth.

When a chord consists of a root, major third, and a perfect fifth it is known as a major triad. When the triad is altered by lowering the major third one half-step, it becomes a minor triad. The examples below are chords that have altered intervals.

Major Chords

The first (or tonic), third, and fifth degree of a major scale make up the notes of a major triad or chord. In the example below, a C major scale is used.

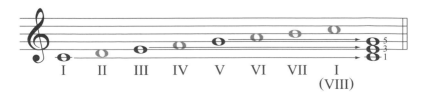

Seventh Chords

The seventh chord is made up of four notes; the first, third, fifth, and the flatted seventh.

add a flatted seventh

Minor Chords

To construct a minor triad simply lower the third of a major chord.

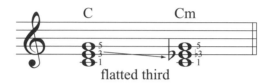

flatted third

Minor Seventh Chords

The minor seventh chord consists of four notes; the first, flatted third, fifth, and flatted seventh.

add a flatted seventh

Augmented Chords

The augmented chord is a major triad with a raised fifth. The plus sign (+) or "aug." are often used as an abbreviation for the augmented chord.

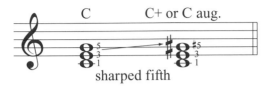

sharped fifth

Diminished Chord

To construct a diminished chord simply flat the fifth of a minor chord. To make a diminished seventh, double flat the seventh degree as well as the fifth. The degree symbol (○) is often used to abbreviate the diminished chord.

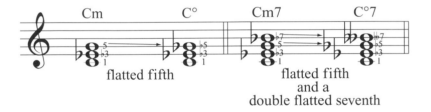

flatted fifth   flatted fifth
                          and a
                    double flatted seventh

Major Sixth Chord

The major sixth chord is major triad with the sixth added.

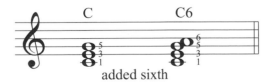

added sixth

Major Seventh Chord

The major seventh chord is a major triad with the seventh added.

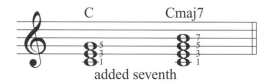

added seventh

Inversions

Inversions are produced by arranging the intervals of a chord in a non-sequential order. A triad that has its tonic as the bottom or lowest tone is said to be in *root position.* A triad with a third as the bottom or lowest tone is in the *first inversion,* and a triad with a fifth as the bottom or lowest tone is in the *second inversion.* As the chords become more complex—such as sixths, sevenths, *etc.*—there will be more possible inversions.

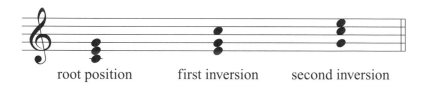

root position   first inversion   second inversion

Note that when inverting more complex chords the inversion may actually become a completely different chord.

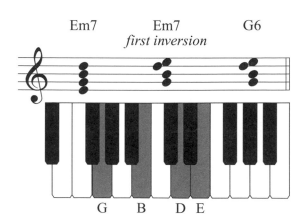

Enharmonic Spelling

Two notes that sound the same but are written differently are said to be *enharmonic* to one another. An example of this is the enharmonic pair C♯ and D♭: these are just two different ways of representing the same tone. The choice of which spelling of a note to use is based on the harmonic function of the tone in the music.

Take a look at the example below. The first chord sounds like a D♭ minor triad, but it is difficult to recognize from the way it is spelled. The second spelling shown is unquestionably easier to read at a glance because it looks like a triad.

The following is a list of all major, minor, augmented, and diminished triads and major sixth, seventh, and major seventh chords.

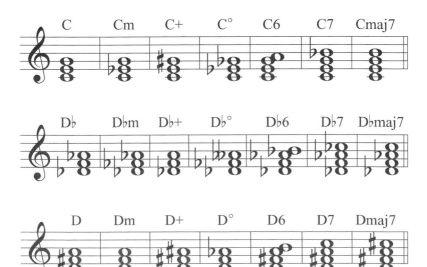

65

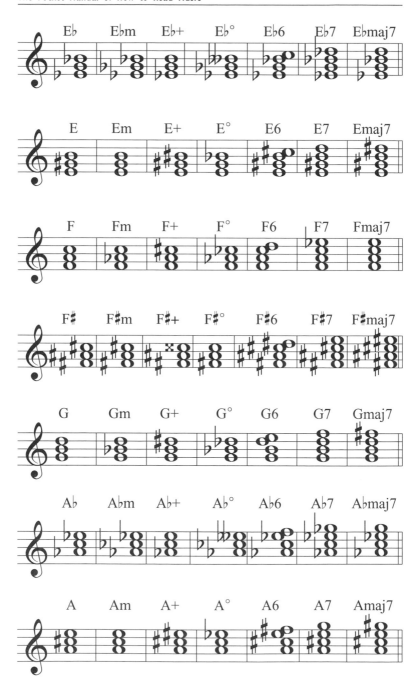

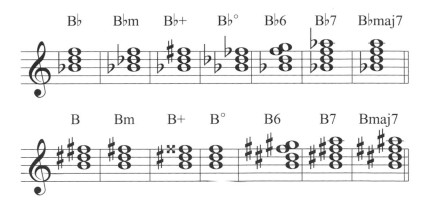

Dynamics

How high or low a tone sounds is described by pitch. How long
the tone is held is a function of its duration. When you talk about
the loudness or softness of a tone, you are discussing *dynamics*.
Dynamic markings in a musical piece tell the player when to
play loudly or softly or in between.
Dynamic markings may be in any language, but they are most
often given in Italian. The chart below shows the commonly
used terms along with their symbols and definitions.

ppp	=	Pianississimo	=	as soft as possible
pp	=	Pianissimo	=	very soft
p	=	Piano	=	soft
mp	=	Mezzo piano	=	moderately soft
mf	=	Mezzo forte	=	moderately loud
f	=	Forte	=	loud
ff	=	Fortissimo	=	very loud
fff	=	Fortississimo	=	as loud as possible

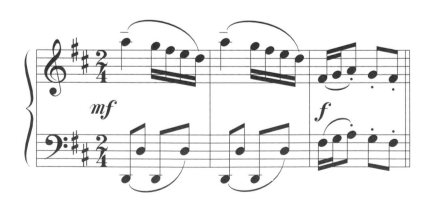

There are times that you will want the volume to gradually become louder or softer. When volume is increased the process is called *crescendo*, abbreviated *cresc.* When the volume is decreased it is called either *decrescendo* or *diminuendo;* and *dim.* is used as an abbreviation for both.

There are times, in music, when a series of notes, or a phrase, needs to have a volume increase or decrease. The crescendo and decrescendo symbols are used for just such occurrences. Sometimes these markings stand alone, meaning the increase or decrease is left up to the player, but in other cases a dynamic marking is placed at the end of the symbol to let the player know how loud or soft to be at the end of the phrase.

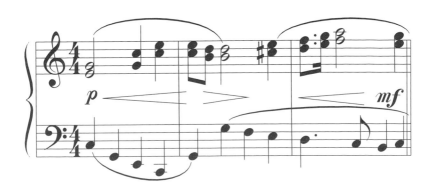

Tempo

The speed of music—how fast or slow a piece is played—is called *tempo*. Tempo gives music its life; by strategically changing speeds a whole range of feelings can be expressed—from a slow emotional passage to a fast dramatic passage that ends with a sudden stop. Specific terms, usually in Italian, are placed at the beginning of a piece to instruct the musician as to the correct speed for performance of the piece. The following columns list some commonly used Italian terms for various tempos.

Grave	solemnly, slowly
Largo	very slow, stately
Larghetto	quite slow, broad
Lento	slowly
Adagio	slowly, with expression
Adagietto	slightly faster than Adagio
Andantino	usually slower than Andante, sometimes faster
Andante	moving, walking speed
Moderato	moderately, medium speed
Allegretto	moving, but slower than Allegro
Allegro	lively, animated
Vivace	animated, faster than Allegro
Vivo	lively, brisk
Presto	fast
Prestissimo	very fast

The following terms are used for both tempo and dynamics.

Allargando	growing broader and slower
Calando	gradually softer and slower
Marcia	march
Morendo	fading away
Perdendo	getting lost, fading away
Sminuendo	slower and softer
Smorzando	fading away

Once a the tempo is established a composer can use other terms in a piece to inform the musician of tempo changes. *Rallentando* (abbreviated *rall.*) and *ritardando* (abbreviated *rit.* or *ritard.*) are used to tell the musician to slow the tempo down. *Accelerando* tells the musician that the tempo is to be increased. The term *a tempo* informs the musician that the piece is to return to its original tempo.

Rubato, Italian for "robbed," is a term that lets the musician decide the tempo of certain passages. Usually melodic tones or emotional chords are held out while the tempo is sped up on the remaining notes to even out the rhythm. When the composer uses the term *tempo commodo* the musician decides what tempo to use for the piece. The following terms may also be used for slowing down or speeding up tempos in musical pieces.

Slowing Down

Allargando	slowing and broadening
Calando	gradually slower and softer
Meno mosso	less speed
Meno moto	less movement
Molto meno mosso	with much less speed
Morendo	dying away by degrees
Slargando	gradually slower
Slentando	slackening, slowing down
Sminuendo	slower and softer
Smorzando	slower and softer
Strascinando	gradually slower
Tardando	gradually slower

Speeding Up

Affrettando	hurrying, sometimes temporarily
Doppio movimento	twice as fast
Incalzando	with more warmth and fervor
Più mosso	more movement
Più moto	more movement
Stringendo	hurrying, speeding up
Veloce	greatly increased speed
Velocissimo	with great velocity

Metronome Markings

When a musical composition requires that exact tempos be specified, the composer may use *metronome markings*. A metronome is a device that "ticks out" a steady beat and can be adjusted to a precise tempo setting—a specific number of beats per minute. Metronomes can be either mechanical or electronic. The mechanical metronome is usually in a pyramid shaped container with a key on the side—to wind it up—and a center shaft with a moveable weight that slides up or down to adjust to the desired tempo. The electronic metronome can be made of plastic or metal with an off/on switch and some type of knob that can set the tempo. Another type of electronic metronome can be found in most music sequencing programs for the computer.

The metronome marking is usually found notated above the time signature and it indicates how many beats a minute a specific beat value receives. In the example below, a quarter note receives 60 beats per minute, which is equivalent to Andante.

Time signatures based on half, dotted quarter, or eighth note values use these values for the metronome marking. The examples below are each designated to be played at 90 beats per minute; this would be Moderato.

The following chart shows how metronome markings relate to the standard Italian, English, French, and German tempo markings. Remember that all of these terms are open to the interpretation of the performer, and so the metronome equivalents shown are necessarily approximations.

Table of Tempo Indications

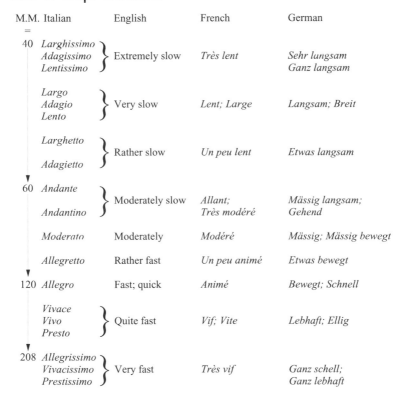

M.M. =	Italian	English	French	German
40	*Larghissimo* *Adagissimo* *Lentissimo*	Extremely slow	*Très lent*	*Sehr langsam* *Ganz langsam*
	Largo *Adagio* *Lento*	Very slow	*Lent; Large*	*Langsam; Breit*
	Larghetto *Adagietto*	Rather slow	*Un peu lent*	*Etwas langsam*
60	*Andante* *Andantino*	Moderately slow	*Allant;* *Très modéré*	*Mässig langsam;* *Gehend*
	Moderato	Moderately	*Modéré*	*Mässig; Mässig bewegt*
	Allegretto	Rather fast	*Un peu animé*	*Etwas bewegt*
120	*Allegro*	Fast; quick	*Animé*	*Bewegt; Schnell*
	Vivace *Vivo* *Presto*	Quite fast	*Vif; Vite*	*Lebhaft; Ellig*
208	*Allegrissimo* *Vivacissimo* *Prestissimo*	Very fast	*Très vif*	*Ganz schell;* *Ganz lebhaft*

Expression

Music is an emotional and extremely expressive art form. Many composers try to convey to the musician what emotion or expression to think of while playing the piece of music. The following are Italian and English terms used to express a wide range of emotions.

Affanato	sad, distressed
Affettuoso	tender
Amabile	amiable, gentle
Amorevole	loving, gentle
Animato	animated, spirited
Appassionato	passionate, much feeling
Ardito	boldly
Ardore	with warmth, ardor
Bravura	skill, dexterity
Brillante	sparkling, showy
Brio	vigor, spirit
Calma	quiet, tranquil
Calore	warmth
Cantabile	in a singing style
Capriccioso	capricious, fanciful
Deciso	bold, determined
Dolce	sweet, mild
Dolendo	sorrowful
Espressivo	expressive
Forzando	force, strength
Fuoco	fire
Furioso	furious, wild
Giocoso	playful, humorous
Gioioso	joy, cheer
Intrepido	bold
Maestoso	majestic, stately
Mesto	sad

Misterioso	mysteriously
Nobilemente	grand, lofty, noble
Placido	calm, tranquil
Pomposo	pompous
Preciso	precise, exact
Religioso	religious, devotional
Risoluto	resolute, firm
Robusto	firm, bold
Scherzando	(in a) playful manner
Scherzo	joke
Scioto	easy, free
Semplice	simple, unaffected
Sentimento	sentiment, feeling
Sentito	expressive
Sereno	serene
Spiritoso	spirited
Strepitoso	noisy, boisterous
Teneramente	tenderly, delicately
Tranquillo	tranquil, quiet
Vago	vague, dreamy

Repeat Signs

Repeat signs in music are a type of shorthand for composers. Instead of rewriting whole sections of music these symbols [:||] are used to tell the musician to repeat certain sections of music.

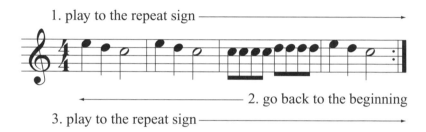

If a composer wants a specific section of music repeated, this symbol [||:] is used to indicate to the musician where the repeated section begins. The musician will play to the [:||], then go back to the [||:] and repeat that section of music.

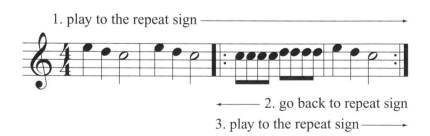

Da capo (pronounced "dah kah'poh") is an Italian phrase that means "from the beginning," and is abbreviated *D.C.*. The *D.C.* marking tells the musician to go back to the beginning of the piece and repeat to the end. The *D.C.* marking can be used just like a single repeat sign.

Dal segno (pronounced "dahl say-nyoh") is an Italian phrase that means "from the sign," and is abbreviated *D.S.*. The *D.S.* marking tells the musician to go back to the *segno* [%] and repeat that section of music to the end.

Alternate Endings

There are times when a composer wants to repeat a certain section of music, but would like to use a different ending. Instead of rewriting the whole section, the composer uses a single repeat and a bracket with the number one over the measure or measures that indicate the *first ending*. The musician will then repeat from the beginning to the first bracket; then skip to the next bracket marked with the number two (or the second ending).

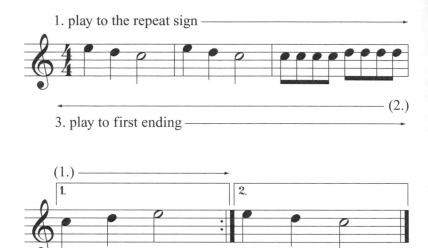

Da capo and *dal segno* also can be used for alternate endings. *D.C. al Coda* tells the musician to go back to the beginning and play the section of music until the coda sign [ɸ] is reached, then skip to the next coda sign and play the coda section to the end.

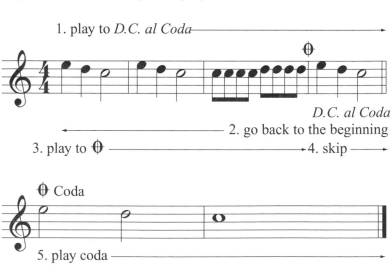

D.S. al Coda tells the musician to go back to the *segno,* then play to the first coda sign, skip to the next coda sign and play the coda section to the end.

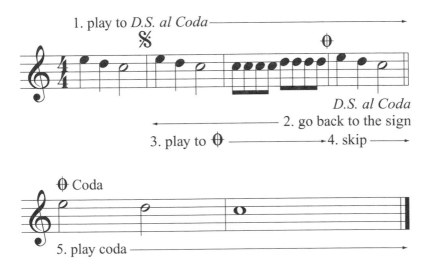

There are two other ways *D.C.* and *D.S.* can be used. They are used in conjunction with the Italian term *Fine* (pronounced "fee'nay") which means "end." *D.C. al Fine* tells the musician to go back to the beginning of the piece and repeat until the *Fine* is reached.

D.S. al Fine tells the musician to go back to the sign and play
until the *Fine* is reached.

Accents

Staccato

One of the most commonly used accent marks is the *staccato*. The staccato mark is a small dot above or below the note head; this indicates that the note is to be played short and abrupt. Generally, the staccato note is held for less than half of the note's value. As you can see by the example below it is easier to read the notes that are staccato than the sixteenth note, sixteenth rest, and eighth note combination.

There is one other staccato mark; it is a small triangle placed above or below the note. This staccato is like the dotted staccato except it is stressed even more.

Accents

All the accent signs in the example below are played with a strong accent and held for their full note value.

sf, *sz*, and *sfz* (abbreviation for *szforzando*) and *rf* (abbreviation for *rinforzando*) are accent marks that indicate a note is to be played with a very strong accent. These symbols are placed below the note head when the stem is up and above when the stem is down.

Articulations

Slur

A *slur* is a curved line, much like a tie, that connects a group of notes together. This indicates that the group of notes is to be played *legato* or smoothly. Although a slur looks like a tie it does not make the group of notes into one note value.

Slurs can also incorporate staccato marks as part of a group of notes. This tells the musician to play the group somewhat detached, but to do so while still playing smoothly.

Phrase Mark

A phrase mark is just like a slur, but it is used on longer passages to indicate the natural punctuation for a musical piece. It can also be used to tell a singer or instrumental player where to take a breath, but it is usually used for phrasing the melody of a piece.

Ornaments

Grace Note

The *grace note* is a small note that comes before a regular note. The grace note is usually a cue-sized eighth note with a line through its flag and stem.

Most grace notes are unaccented, meaning the note is played as quick as possible before the natural occurrence of the beat. The value of the grace note is subtracted from the value of the previous note.

The *accented grace note* or *appoggiatura* is played on the beat and its value is subtracted from the following note.

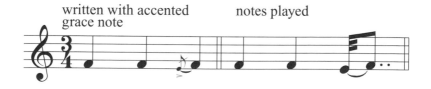

Grace notes can be written using different values other than an eighth note and are usually in groups of two, three, or four notes. These grouped grace notes are usually unaccented and their value is subtracted from the previous note. Groups of two or three are beamed with two beams (like a sixteenth-note grouping), and groups of four or more are beamed with three beams (like a thirty-second-note grouping).

Trill

The *trill* symbol [*tr*] tells the musician alternate between the written note and the note above it—as determined by the diatonic scale—as rapidly and evenly as possible. The lower note is called the *principal note* and the second note is called the *auxiliary.* The trill lasts for the duration of the note value.

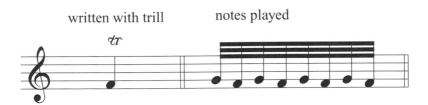

When longer notes are used the trill symbol is accompanied by a wavy line which extents to the end of the barline.

The auxiliary note of a trill need not be the next scale step above the principal note. An accidental can be placed next to the trill sign to tell the musician which note to play.

Tremolo

The *tremolo* is written as two half notes beamed together and played as a series of alternating eighth notes. When the half notes are beamed with two beams, the notes are played as alternating sixteenth notes. Tremolos can be either beamed or the beams can be placed in between the two notes. When a tremolo is made up of one or two beams it is called a *measured tremolo*. Below are some examples of different types of tremolos.

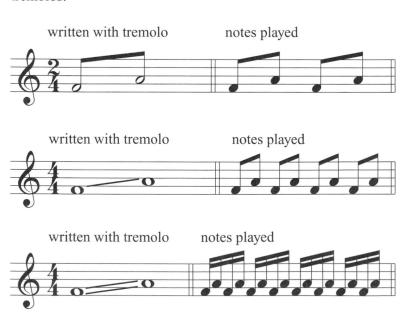

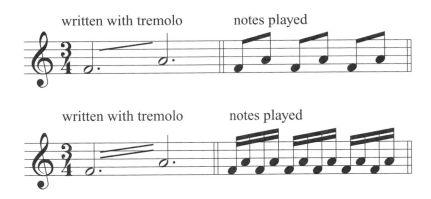

When a tremolo has three beams, the notes are played as alternating thirty-second notes or as fast as the musician can play them. This type of tremolo is called an *unmeasured tremolo.*

Instrumentalists and string players encounter a type of tremolo where the three beams are drawn through the stem. This tells the musician to repeat the note as a series of thirty-second notes, or simply as fast as possible.

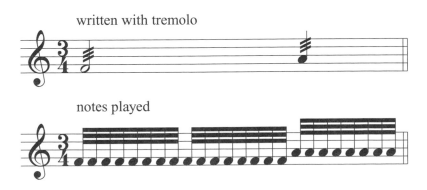

Turns

When a *turn symbol* [∿] is placed over a note, a specific series of notes is to be played as in the example below.

When the turn symbol is placed *after* the note, the turn is executed on the second half of the beat.

When the *inverted turn symbol* [∾] is used, the turn starts on the note below the designated note.

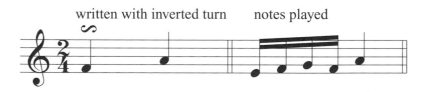

When an inverted turn symbol is placed after the note, the turn is executed on the second half of the beat.

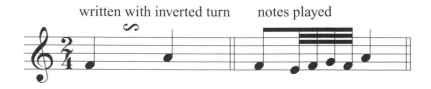

Mordent

The *mordent symbol* [⌇] is a grace note consisting of a single rapid alternation between the principal and the above auxiliary note. This mordent is sometimes called an *upper mordent.*

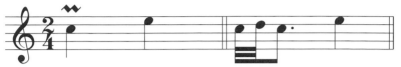

This mordent symbol [⌇] is called a *lower mordent* and is the same as the upper mordent, but the alternation is between the principal and the auxiliary note below.

Turns and mordents are not usually found in popular music. These ornaments appear mainly in music from the baroque and classical periods.

Transposition

It is sometimes necessary to rewrite a piece of music in a different key. This is known as *transposition*. It is important to have a thorough understanding of intervals before tackling transposition. Let's transpose the example below from the key of G to the key of B.

First start with a new staff and write in the key signature for B—five sharps F♯, C♯, G♯, D♯, and A♯. Then write in the time signature which will remain the same as the original example (¾). Notice in the original example, in the key of G, that the starting note is G, so the new starting note for the key of B will be B, which is up a major third (four half-steps). Now transpose every note up a major third. In the original example the first three notes are the first, third, and fifth degrees of the G scale, consequently the first three notes of the transposed example should be the first, third, and fifth degrees of the B scale. This is what the transposed piece should look like.

The example above is fairly straightforward. Transposition can be confusing when accidentals are involved. Look at the example below. The original piece is in A minor and the transposed piece is in F minor. Notice the placement of the accidentals in the F minor piece as compared to the A minor piece.

Transposing Instruments

Certain instruments, called *transposing instruments,* require music written for them to be transposed. Here is an example of how to transpose music for a B♭ trumpet.

Start with the music written in *concert pitch; i.e.,* the way it would be written for the piano or any other *nontransposing instrument* in the key of C.

The piano sounds the same as it is written

The B♭ trumpet sound one whole-step lower than it is written. If the trumpet played the above example as written, it would sound one whole-tone lower and come out in the key of B♭.

The B♭ trumpet as written

The B♭ trumpet as it sounds

In order to write out the melody so that it sounds in the key of C when played by the trumpet player, you must transpose it up one whole-step to the key of D.

There are many transposing instruments. The following is a list of some of these instruments and the intervals to which they transpose.

Clarinet in A	sounds a minor third lower than written
Clarinet in B♭	sounds a major second lower than written
Trumpet in B♭	sounds a major second lower than written
Cornet in B♭	sounds a major second lower than written
Soprano Saxophone	sounds a major second lower than written
Bass Clarinet	sounds a major ninth (an octave and a major second) lower than written
Tenor Saxophone	sounds a major ninth (an octave and a major second) lower than written
Clarinet in E♭	sounds a minor third higher than written
Alto Clarinet	sounds a major sixth lower than written
Alto Saxophone	sounds a major sixth lower than written
Baritone Saxophone	sounds an octave and a major sixth lower than written
French Horn in F	sounds a perfect fifth lower than written
English Horn in F	sounds a perfect fifth lower than written

There are also instruments that transpose either up or down one octave. These are known as *true transposing* instruments, meaning they transpose by pitch and not by key. For example, the piccolo sounds one octave higher than written and the bass violin, contrabassoon, and guitar sound one octave lower than written.

The piccolo as written

The piccolo as it sounds

The bass violin as written

The bass violin as it sounds

Appendix I
Musical Terms

The instruments listed here are used in both band and orchestra scores. Many of these instruments have optional names and abbreviations. The names in this table are the most widely used, and the abbreviations are the most common.

English	Italian	French	German
Woodwinds	**Legni (or Fiat.)**	**Bois**	**Holzbläser**
Piccolo	Flauto piccolo or Ottavino	Petite Flûte	Kleine Flöte
(Picc.)	(Picc.)	(pte Fl.)	(Kl. Fl.)
Flute(s) (Fl.)	Flauto(-i) (Fl.)	Grande(s) Flûte(s) (Gde Fl.)	Grosse Flöte(n) (Fl.)
Alto Flute (in G) (Alto Fl.)	Flauto contralto (Fl. c'alto)	Flûte alto (en sol) (Fl. alto)	Altflöte (Altfl.)
Oboe (s) (Ob.)	Oboe (-i) (Ob.)	Hautbois (Hb.)	Hoboe (n) (Hob.)
English Horn (E. H.)	Corno inglese (Cor. ingl.)	Cor Anglais (Cor. Ang.)	Englisch Horn (Engl. Hr.)
E♭ Clarinet	Clarinetto piccolo in Mi♭	Petite clarinette en Mi♭	Klarinette in Es
(E♭ Cl.)	(Cl. picc.)	(Pte Cl.)	(Es-Kl.)
Clarinet(s) (Cl.)	Clarinetto(-i) (Cl.)	Clarinette(s) (Cl.)	Klarinette(n) (Kl.)
Alto Clarinet (Alto Cl.)	Clarinetto contralto (Cl. c'alto)	Clarinette alto (Cl. alto)	Altklarinette (Altkl.)
Bass Clarinet (B. Cl.)	Clarinetto basso (Cl. b.)	Clarinette basse (Cl. B.)	Bassklarinette (Basskl.)
Contrabass Clarinet (Cb. Cl.)	Clarinetto contrabasso (Cl. Cb.)	Clarinette contrebasse (Cl. C.B.)	Kontrabass Klarinette (Kb. Kl.)
Bassoon(s) (Bn.)	Fagotto(-i) (Fg.)	Basson(s) (Bon)	Fagott(e) (Fg.)

English	Italian	French	German
Contra or Double Bassoon (C. or D. Bn.)	Contrafagotto (C. fg.)	Contre-basson (C. Bon)	Kontrafagott (Kfg.)
Saxophone(s) (Sax.)	Sassofone(-i) (Sass.)	Saxophone(s) (Sax.)	Saxophon(e) (Sax.)
Brass	**Ottoni**	**Cuivres**	**Blechinstrumente**
Horn (s) (Hn.)	Corno (-i) (Cor.)	Cor (s)	Horn (Hörner) (Hrn.)
Trumpet (s) (Tpt.)	Tromba (-e) (Tr.)	Trompette (s) (Tr.)	Trompete (n) (Tr)
Cornet(s) (Cnt.)	Cornetto(-i) a pistoni (C-a-p.)	Cornet(s) à pistons (C.-à-p.)	Kornett(e) (Kor.)
Bass Trumpet (B. Tpt.)	Tromba bassa (Tr. bassa)	Trompette basse (Tr. basse)	Basstrompete (Basstr.)
Trombone(s) (Tenor) (Tbn.)	Trombone(-i) (tenore(-i)) (Trb.)	Trombone(s) (Trb.)	Posaune(n) (Tenor) (Pos.)
Bass Trombone (B. Tbn.)	Trombone basso (Trb. basso)	Trombone basse (Trb. b.)	Bassposaune (B.-Pos.)
Baritone (Bar.)	Flicorno tenore	Bugle ténor	Tenorhorn
Euphonium	Eufonio	Basse a pistons	Baryton
(Bass) Tuba (Tb.)	Tuba (di bassa) (Tb.)	Tuba (basse) (Tb.)	Tuba or Basstuba (Tb.)
Percussion			
Timpani (Timp.)	Timpani (Timp.)	Timbales (Timb.)	Pauken (Pk.)
Bass Drum (B. Dr.)	Gran cassa (Gr. c.)	Grosse Caisse (Gr. C.)	Grosse Trommel (Gr. Tr.)
Snare Drum (S. Dr.)	Tamburo militare (Tamb.)	Tambour militaire (Tamb.)	Kleine Trommel (Kl. Tr.)
Tenor Drum (T. Dr.)	Tamburo rullante (Tamb. r.)	Caisse roulante Caisse (r.)	Rührtrommel (Rtr.)
Cymbals (Cym.)	Piatti (Ptti.)	Cymbales (Cymb.)	Becken (Beck.)
Suspended Cymbal (Susp. Cym.)	Piatto (sospeso)	Cymbale (suspendue) (Cymb. s.)	Becken (frei)
Antique Cymbals (Ant. Cym.)	Crotali	Cymbales antiques (Cymb. ant.)	Antike Zimbeln (Ant. Zimb.)
Finger Cymbals (Fing. Cym.)	Cimbalini	Cymbales Digitales	Fingerzimbeln

English	Italian	French	German
Gong	Gong	Gong	Gong
Tam-tam	Tam-tam	Tam-tam	Tam-tam
	(Tam.)	(T. T.)	(T.-t.)
Tambourine	Tamburino	Tambour de Basque	Tambourin
(Tamb.)	(Tamb.)	(Tamb. de Basque)	(Tamb.)
Triangle	Triangolo	Triangle	Triangel
(Trgl.)	(Trgl.)	(Trg.)	(Trgl.)
Castanets	Castagnette	Castagnettes	Kastagnetten
(Casts.)	(Cast.)	(Cast.)	(Kast.)
Chimes or Bells	Campane Tubolari	Cloches	Glocken
(Tubular)	(Camp.)		(Glock.)
Glockenspiel or	Campanelli	Carillon or	Glockenspiel
Chime-Bells		Jeu de Timbres	
(Glock.)	(Cmplli.)	(Car. or J. de T.)	(Glsp.)
Bongos	Bongos	Bongos	Bongos
(Bong.)	(Bong.)	(Bong.)	(Bong.)
Claves	Claves	Claves	Claves
Guiro (Rasper)	Raspe	Râpe	Raspel
Maracas	Maracas	Maracas	Maracas
Rattle (Ratchet)	Raganella	Crécelle	Ratsche
Sandpaper Blocks	Ceppi di carta vetro	Blocs a papier	Sandpapierblocke
		de verre	
(Sand. Bl.)			
Siren	Sirena	Sirène	Sirene
Slapstick (Whip)	Frusta	Fouet	Peitsche
Sleighbells	Sonagli	Crelots	(Roll)schellen
Temple Blocks			
(Temp. Bl.)			
Wind Machine	Macchina a venti	Machine à vent	Windmaschine
Wood Block	Cassettina	Blocs de bois	Holzblock
(Wd. Bl.)			
Xylophone	Silofano (or Xilofono)	Xylophone	Xylophon
(Xyl.)	(Sil.)	(Xyl.)	(Xyl.)
Vibraphone	Vibrafono	Vibraphone	Vibraphon
(Vib.)	(Vibraf.)	(Vibraph.)	(Vibraph.)
Marimba	Marimba	Marimba	Marimbaphon

Harp and Keyboard

Harp(s)	Arpa(e)	Harpe(s)	Harfe(n)
(Hp.)	(Arp)	(Hrp.)	(Hrf.)

English	Italian	French	German
Celesta (Cel.)	Celesta (Cel.)	Célesta (Cel.)	Celesta (Cel.)
Harpsichord (Hpscd.)	Clavicembalo (Cemb.)	Clavecin (Clav.)	Kielflügel (Kielfl.)
Organ (Org.)	Organo (Org.)	Orgue (Org.)	Orgel (Org.)
Piano (Pn.)	Pianoforte (Pf.)	Piano (Pn.)	Klavier (Klav.)

Strings

English	Italian	French	German
Violin (s) (Vn.)	Violino (-i) (Vl.)	Violon (s) (Von)	Violine (n) or Geige(n) (Vl.)
Viola (Va.)	Viola(-e) (Va.)	Alto(s) (Alt.)	Bratsche(n) (Br.)
Violoncello or Cello(s) (Vc.)	Violoncello (-i) (Vcl.)	Violoncelle (s) (Vc.)	Violoncello (-e) (Vc.)
Bass (es) or Double bass (es) or Contrabass (es) (B., Db., Cb.)	Contrabasso- (i) (Cb.)	Contrebasse (s) (Cb.)	Kontrabass (bass) (Kb.)

Voices

English	Italian	French	German
Soprano (s) (S.)	Soprano (-i) (S.)	Soprano (s) (S.)	Sopran (c) (S.)
Alto(s) (A.)	Alto(-i) (A.)	Contralto(es) (C.)	Alt(e) (A.)
Tenor (s) (T)	Tenore (-i) (T)	Ténor (es) (T)	Tenor (Tenöre) (T.)
Baritone(s) (Bar.)	Baritono(-i) (Bar.)	Baritone(s) (Bar.)	Baryton(e) (Bar.)
Bass(es) (B)	Basso(-i) (B)	Basse(s) (B.)	Bass (Bässe) (B.)

Degrees of the Scale

English	Italian	French	German
Major	Maggiore	Majeur	Dur
Minor	Minore	Mineur	Moll
C flat	Do bemolle	Ut (Do) bémol	Ces
C	Do	Ut (Do)	C
C sharp	Do diesis	Ut (Do) dièse	Cis
D flat	Re bemolle	Re bémol	Des
D	Re	Re	D

English	Italian	French	German
D sharp	Re diesis	Re dièse	Dis
E flat	Mi bemolle	Mi bémol	Es
E	Mi	Mi	E
E sharp	Mi diesis	Mi dièse	Eis
F flat	Fa bemolle	Fa bémol	Fes
F	Fa	Fa	F
F sharp	Fa diesis	Fa dièse	Fis
G flat	Sol bemolle	Sol bémol	Ces
C	Sol	Sol	C
C sharp	Sol diesis	Sol dièse	Cis
A flat	La bemolle	La bémol	As
A	La	La	A
A sharp	La diesis	La dièse	Ais
B flat	Si bemolle	Si bémol	B
B	Si	Si	H
B sharp	Si diesis	Si dièse	His

Frequently Used Directions for Instruments

all	tutti	tout	alle
half (section)	la metà	la moitié	die Hälfte
desk or stand	leggio	pupitre	Pult
a2	a2	à2	zu 2
unison	unisono	unis	einfach (or zusammen)
divided	divisi	divise	geteilt
div. by 3's	div. a 3	div. à 3	dreifach (or zu 3)
div. by 4's	div. a 4	div. à 4	vierfach (or zu 4)
string	corda	corde	Saite
with mute(s)	con sordino(-i)	avec sourdine(s)	mit Dämpfer(n)
remove mute(s)	via sordino(-i)	otez le(s) sourdine(s)	Dämpfer(n) weg
without mute(s)	senza sordino(-i)	sans sourdine(s)	ohne Dämpfer(n)
at the bridge	sul ponticello	sur le chevalet	am Steg
near the sounding board		près de la table	
over the fingerboard	sul tasto	sur la touche	am Griffbrett

English	Italian	French	German
at the point of the bow	a punte d'arco	au pointe d'archet	an der Spitze
at the frog	al tallone	au talon	am Frosche
in the ordinary manner	modo ordinario	mode ordinaire	gewöhnlich
harmonic	armonico	harmonique	Flageolett
natural	naturale	naturel	natürlich
open	aperto(-i)	ouvert(s)	offen
stopped	chiuso(-i)	bouché(s)	gestopft
brassy	chiuse	cuivré	schmetternd
hard stick(s)	bachetta(e) di legno	baguette(s) en bois	mit Holzschlägel(n)
soft stick(s)	bachetta(e) di spugna	baguette(s) d'éponge	mit Schwamm-schlägel(n)
change___ to___	___muta in ___	changez___ en___	___nach___ umstimmen
bells in the air	campagne in aria	pavillons en l'air	Schalltrichter auf

Appendix II
Scales

Major Scales

Key of C

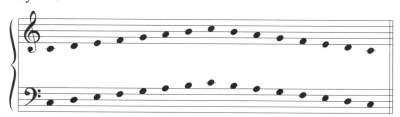

Key of G

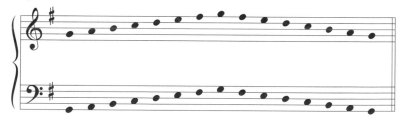

Key of D

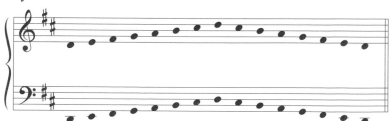

Key of A

Key of E

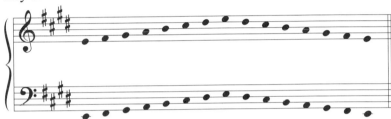

Key of B

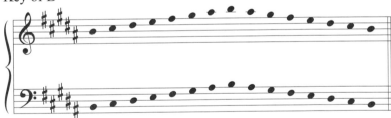

Key of F♯

Key of C#

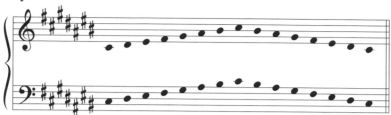

Key of F

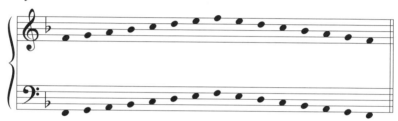

Key of Bb

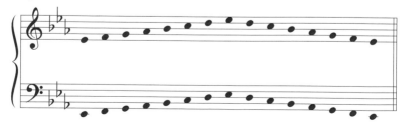

Key of Eb

Key of A♭

Key of D♭

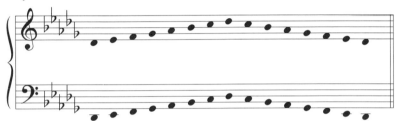

Key of G♭

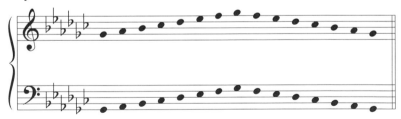

Key of C♭

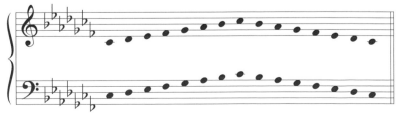

Natural Minor Scales

A natural minor *(Aeolian)*

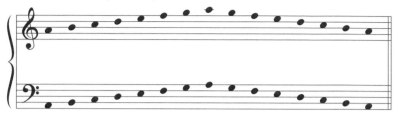

E natural minor *(Aeolian)*

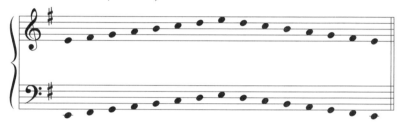

B natural minor *(Aeolian)*

F♯ natural minor *(Aeolian)*

C# natural minor *(Aeolian)*

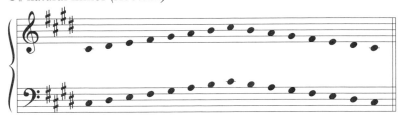

G# natural minor *(Aeolian)*

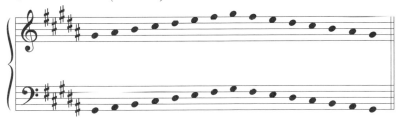

D# natural minor *(Aeolian)*

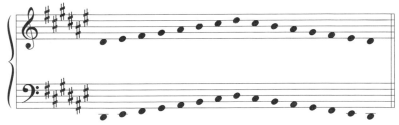

A# natural minor *(Aeolian)*

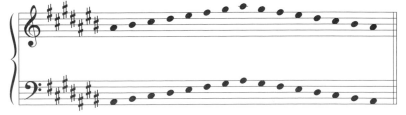

D natural minor *(Aeolian)*

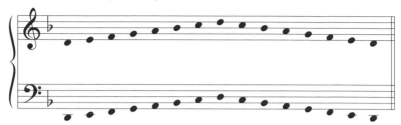

G natural minor *(Aeolian)*

C natural minor *(Aeolian)*

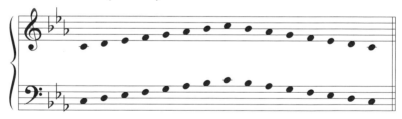

F natural minor *(Aeolian)*

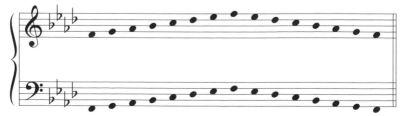

Bb natural minor *(Aeolian)*

Eb natural minor *(Aeolian)*

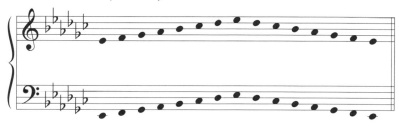

Ab natural minor *(Aeolian)*

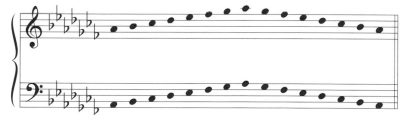

Harmonic Minor Scales

A harmonic minor

E harmonic minor

B harmonic minor

F# harmonic minor

C# harmonic minor

G# harmonic minor

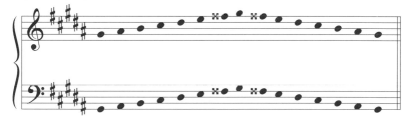

D# harmonic minor

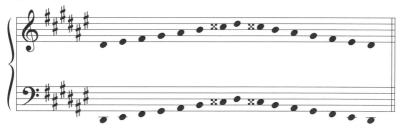

A# harmonic minor

D harmonic minor

G harmonic minor

C harmonic minor

F harmonic minor

B♭ harmonic minor

E♭ harmonic minor

A♭ harmonic minor

Melodic Minor

A melodic minor *(ascending)*

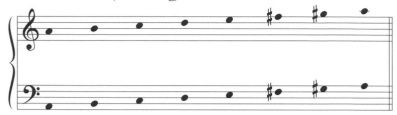

A melodic minor *(descending)*

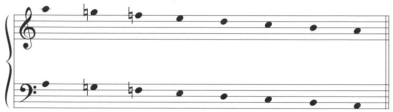

E melodic minor *(ascending)*

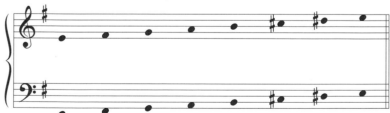

E melodic minor *(descending)*

B melodic minor *(ascending)*

B melodic minor *(descending)*

F♯ melodic minor *(ascending)*

F♯ melodic minor *(descending)*

C# melodic minor *(ascending)*

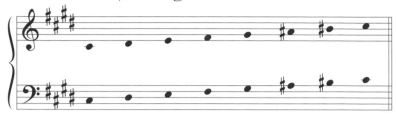

C# melodic minor *(descending)*

G# melodic minor *(ascending)*

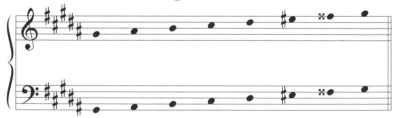

G# melodic minor *(descending)*

D♯ melodic minor *(ascending)*

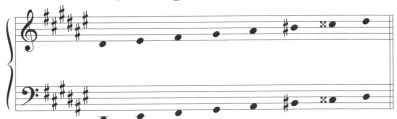

D♯ melodic minor *(descending)*

A♯ melodic minor *(ascending)*

A♯ melodic minor *(descending)*

D melodic minor *(ascending)*

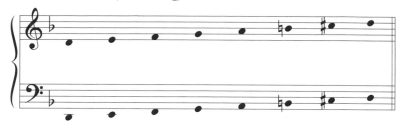

D melodic minor *(descending)*

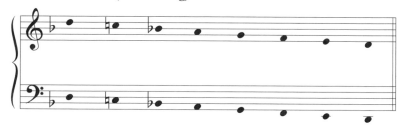

G melodic minor *(ascending)*

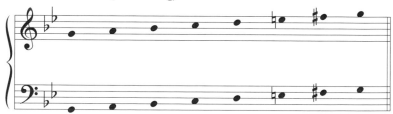

G melodic minor *(descending)*

C melodic minor *(ascending)*

C melodic minor *(descending)*

F melodic minor *(ascending)*

F melodic minor *(descending)*

Bb melodic minor *(ascending)*

Bb melodic minor *(descending)*

Eb melodic minor *(ascending)*

Eb melodic minor *(descending)*

Ab melodic minor *(ascending)*

Ab melodic minor *(descending)*

Dorian Scales

D Dorian

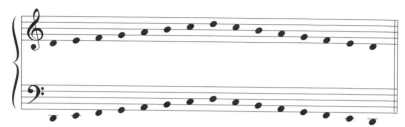

A Dorian

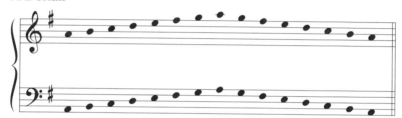

E Dorian

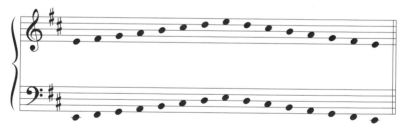

B Dorian

F# Dorian

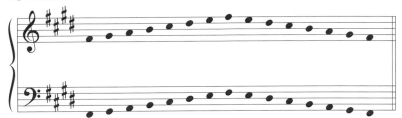

C# Dorian

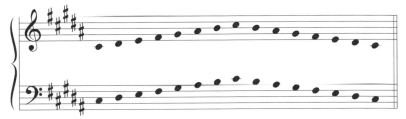

G# Dorian

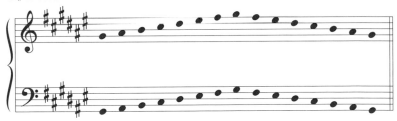

D# Dorian

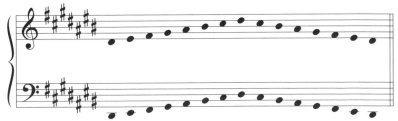

G Dorian

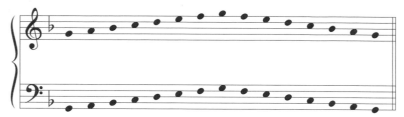

C Dorian

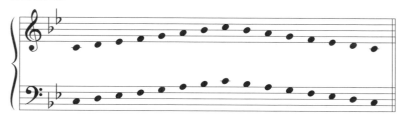

F Dorian

B♭ Dorian

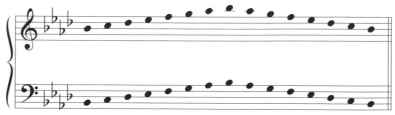

E♭ Dorian

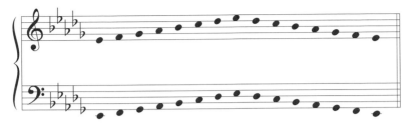

A♭ Dorian

D♭ Dorian

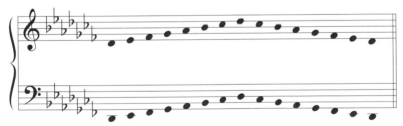

Phrygian Scales

E Phrygian

B Phrygian

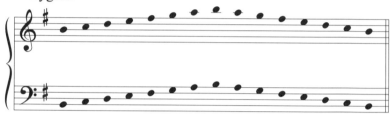

F# Phrygian

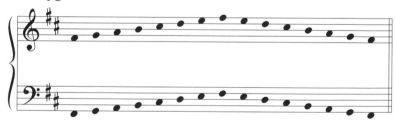

C# Phrygian

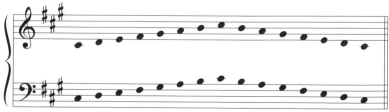

G# Phrygian

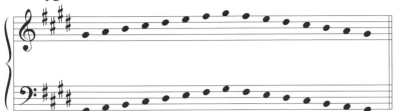

D# Phrygian

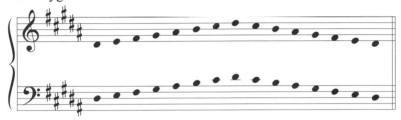

A# Phrygian

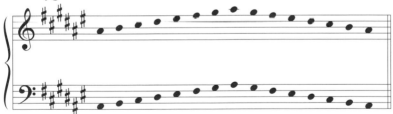

E# Phrygian

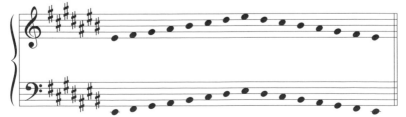

A Phrygian

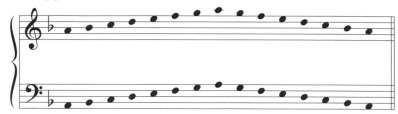

D Phrygian

G Phrygian

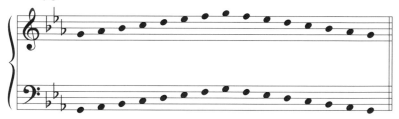

C Phrygian

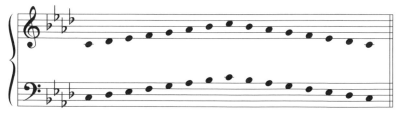

F Phrygian

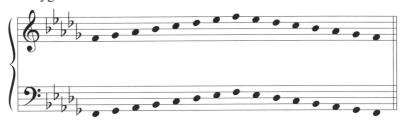

B♭ Phrygian

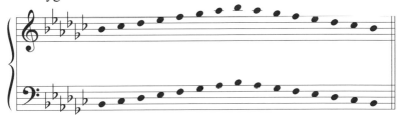

E♭ Phrygian

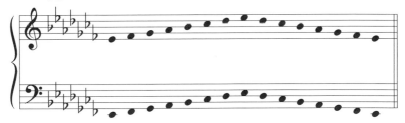

Lydian Scales

F Lydian

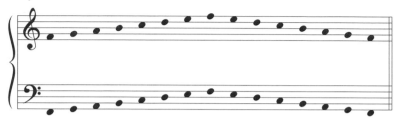

C Lydian

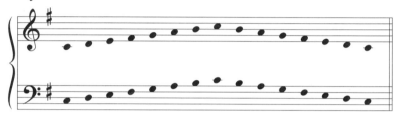

G Lydian

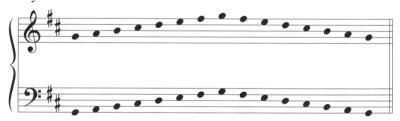

D Lydian

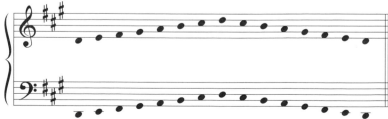

A Lydian

E Lydian

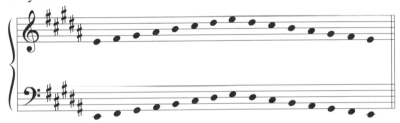

B Lydian

F# Lydian

B♭ Lydian

E♭ Lydian

A♭ Lydian

D♭ Lydian

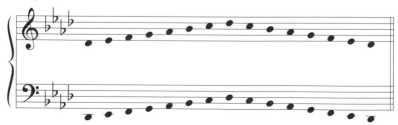

Gb Lydian

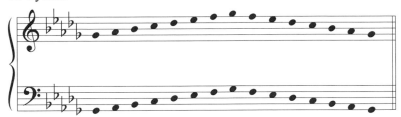

Cb Lydian

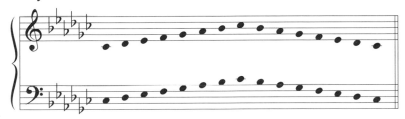

Fb Lydian

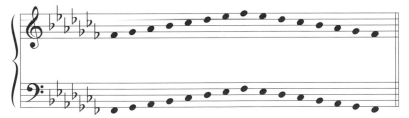

Lydian Flat-Seven

F Lydian flat-seven

C Lydian flat-seven

G Lydian flat-seven

D Lydian flat-seven

A Lydian flat-seven

E Lydian flat-seven

B Lydian flat-seven

F# Lydian flat-seven

B♭ Lydian flat-seven

E♭ Lydian flat-seven

A♭ Lydian flat-seven

D♭ Lydian flat-seven

Gb Lydian flat-seven

Cb Lydian flat-seven

Fb Lydian flat-seven

Mixolydian

G Mixolydian

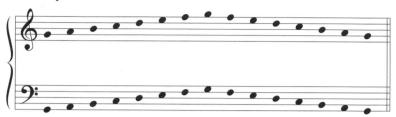

D Mixolydian

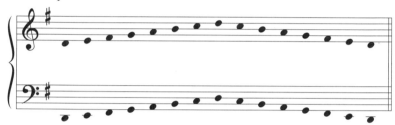

A Mixolydian

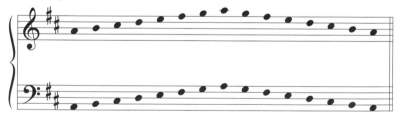

E Mixolydian

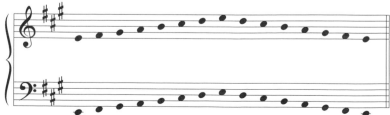

B Mixolydian

F# Mixolydian

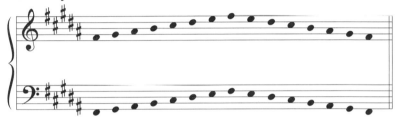

C# Mixolydian

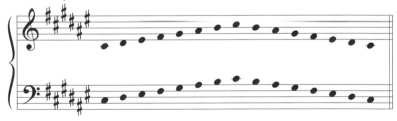

G# Mixolydian

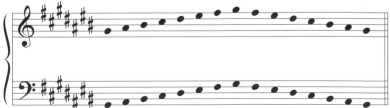

C Mixolydian

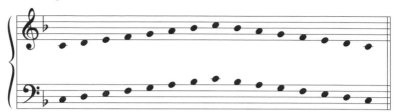

F Mixolydian

B♭ Mixolydian

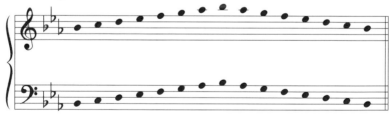

E♭ Mixolydian

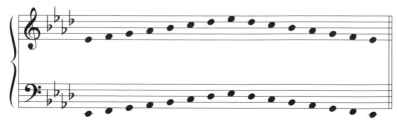

A♭ Mixolydian

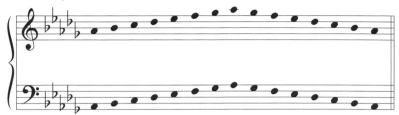

D♭ Mixolydian

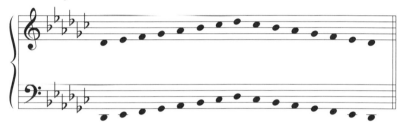

G♭ Mixolydian

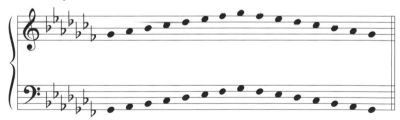

Locrian

B Locrian

F# Locrian

C# Locrian

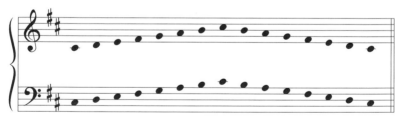

G# Locrian

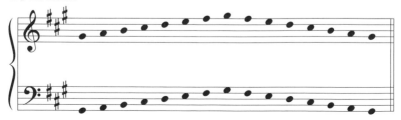

D# Locrian

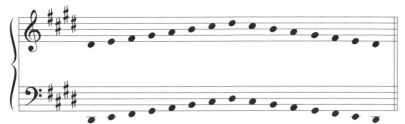

A# Locrian

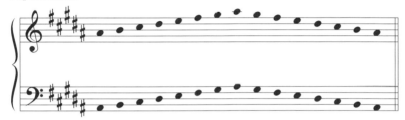

E# Locrian

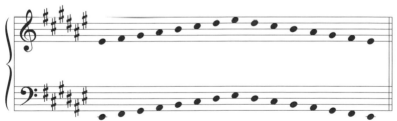

B# Locrian

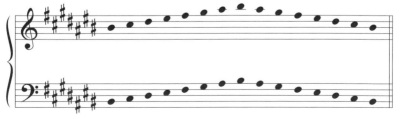

E Locrian

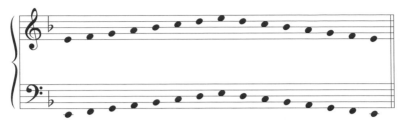

A Locrian

D Locrian

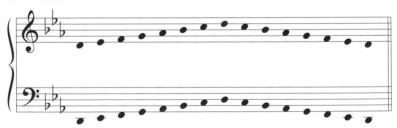

G Locrian

C Locrian

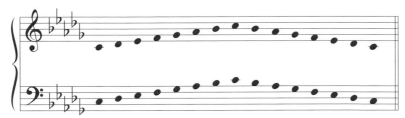

F Locrian

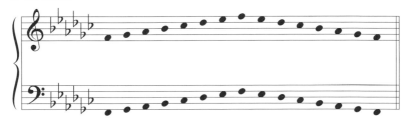

B♭ Locrian

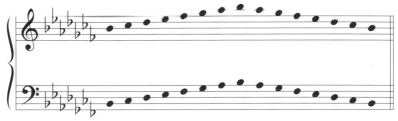

Major Pentatonic Scales

C pentatonic major

G pentatonic major

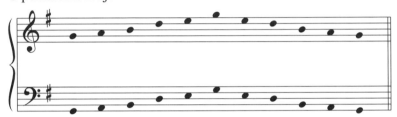

D pentatonic major

A pentatonic major

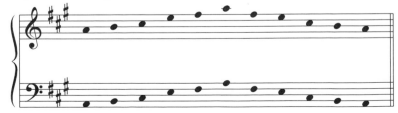

E pentatonic major

B pentatonic major

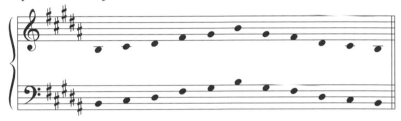

F# pentatonic major

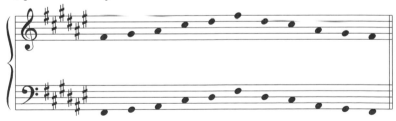

C# pentatonic major

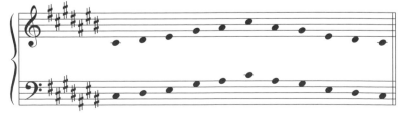

F pentatonic major

B♭ pentatonic major

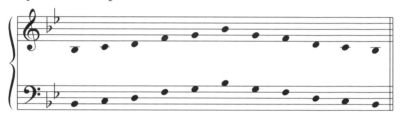

E♭ pentatonic major

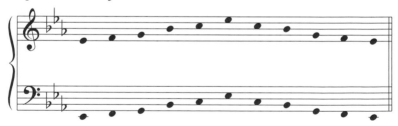

A♭ pentatonic major

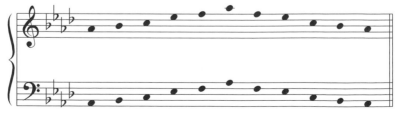

Db pentatonic major

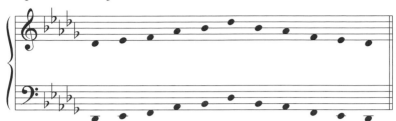

Gb pentatonic major

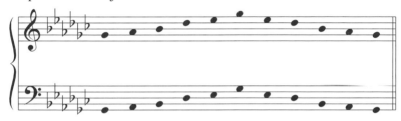

Cb pentatonic major

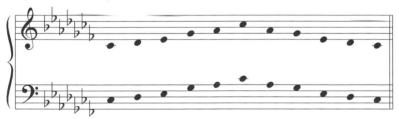

Minor Pentatonic Scales

A pentatonic minor

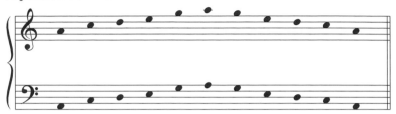

E pentatonic minor

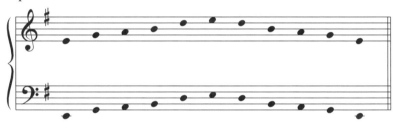

B pentatonic minor

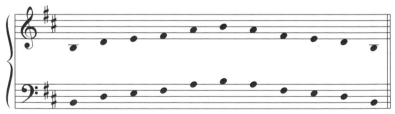

F# pentatonic minor

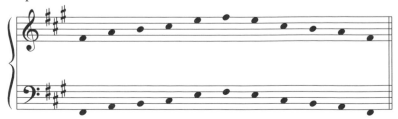

C# pentatonic minor

G# pentatonic minor

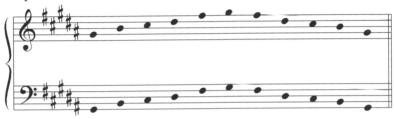

D# pentatonic minor

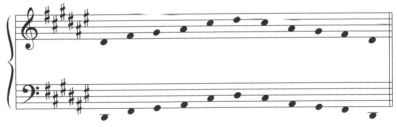

A# pentatonic minor

D pentatonic minor

G pentatonic minor

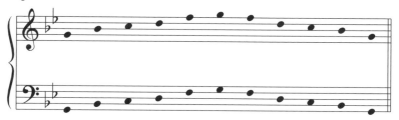

C pentatonic minor

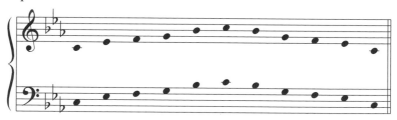

F pentatonic minor

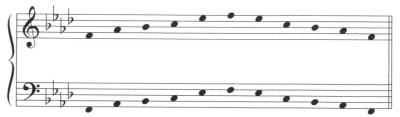

B♭ pentatonic minor

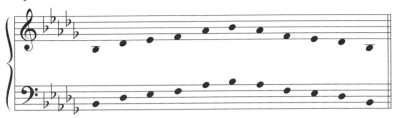

E♭ pentatonic minor

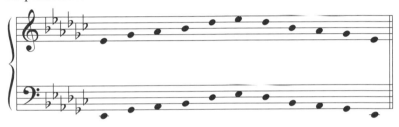

A♭ pentatonic minor

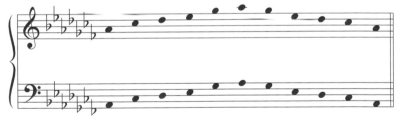

Blues Scales

C blues

G blues

D blues

A blues

E blues

B blues

F# blues

C# blues

F blues

B♭ blues

E♭ blues

A♭ blues

Db blues

Gb blues

Cb blues

Whole Tone Scales

C whole tone

G whole tone

D whole tone

A whole tone

E whole tone

B whole tone

F♯ whole tone

C♯ whole tone

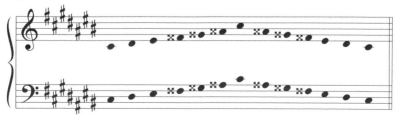

F whole tone

B♭ whole tone

E♭ whole tone

A♭ whole tone

Db whole tone

Gb whole tone

Cb whole tone

Appendix III
Ranges of Instruments and Voices

Piccolo

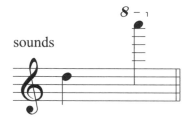

Flute

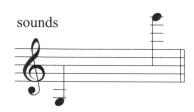

Alto Flute in G

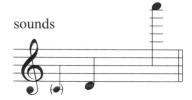

Bass Flute

Oboe

sounds  written

English Horn

sounds  written

Bassoon

sounds  written

Double Bassoon

sounds 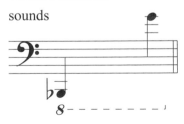 written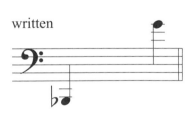

Clarinet in B♭

sounds  written

Clarinet in A

sounds   written

Alto Clarinet in E♭

sounds   written

Bass Clarinet in B♭

sounds   written

Soprano Saxophone

sounds   written

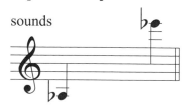 

Alto Saxophone in E♭

sounds   written

Tenor Saxophone in B♭

sounds   written

Baritone Saxophone in E♭

sounds   written

Bass Saxophone in B♭

sounds   written

French Horn in F

sounds   written

Trumpet in B♭

sounds   written

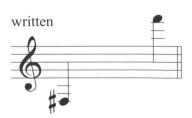

163

Tenor Trombone in B♭

sounds 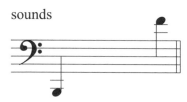   written

Bass Trombone

sounds   written

Tuba (BB♭)

sounds    written

Euphonium in B♭

sounds    written

Violin

sounds    written

Viola

sounds

written

Violoncello

sounds

written

Contrabass

sounds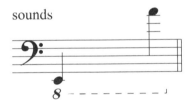

written

Harp

sounds

written

Guitar

sounds

written

Organ
non-transposing

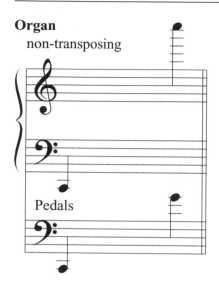

Pedals

Piano
non-transposing

Harpsichord
non-transposing

Celesta

sounds

written

Timpani

sounds

written

Vibraphone

sounds

written

Marimba

sounds

written

Xylophone

sounds

written

Orchestra bells (glockenspiel)

sounds 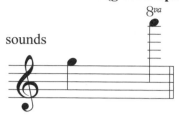 written

Chimes (tubular bells)

sounds  written

Voices
Soprano

sounds  written

Contralto (alto)

sounds  written

Tenor

sounds  written

Baritone (bass I)

sounds  written

Bass (bass II)

sounds  written

4039